RECONNECTED

Moving from Roommates to Soulmates

in Your Marriage

DR. GREG AND ERIN SMALLEY

Tyndale House Publishers
Carol Stream, Illinois

FOCUS ON THE FAMILY®

Contents

CHAPTER 1

In Love with a Stranger

I don't know where we went wrong. But,
the feeling's gone and I just can't get it back.

GORDON LIGHTFOOT

"If You Could Read My Mind"

"I FEEL COMPLETELY disconnected and alone. It's like we're living separate lives under the same roof. We're in a rut as a couple. I love you and I'm committed to our marriage, but I feel like we're nothing more than married roommates."

These were the words I (Erin) spoke during a very frustrating season of our marriage. Brutal, right? Especially since we were supposed to be the marriage *experts*. I had a master's degree in counseling, and Greg had a doctorate in marriage and family. We were both marriage counselors. We'd written five books (at the time) on how to have a thriving marriage—one was even titled *The Marriage You've Always Dreamed Of*. We taught marriage seminars around the world. We counseled couples on the brink of divorce. And yet I was telling Greg that our relationship had faded into the friend zone. Talk about irony.

Erin's words cut deep into my (Greg) heart. It was like she'd taken her diamond wedding ring and used it to carve the words *failure* and *fraud* on my forehead as I stood there staring blankly at her revelation.

But our marriage wasn't always this way. Like you, we started off madly in love. We had big dreams and were ready to take on the world 'til death do us part. In the beginning, our relationship felt more like a fairy tale than a nightmare.

Several months before Erin and I got married, I invited her to help me move from Phoenix to Denver. I wanted her to see where she would be living the following year. Since we hoped to cover those 850 miles in a single day, we planned to meet at my parents' house at about five a.m. and drive until we reached Denver.

By the time Erin arrived, I had loaded a U-Haul truck (equipped with a stick shift, which I'd never driven) and hitched my car to the towing bar behind the trailer. Erin and I said goodbye to my parents and excitedly set off on our adventure.

As I pulled out of the driveway, I accidentally popped the clutch and caused the rental truck to lurch forward. Erin nervously looked at me, smiling. "That's normal," I reassured her. "Stick shift trucks tend to drive rough at the start." As if I knew!

Rumbling down the street, I glanced in the side mirror . . . and saw my dad frantically chasing us, waving his arms.

"What do I do?" I asked Erin, rolling my eyes. "He's running after me! And he's a marathon runner. He can chase us for at least 26.2 miles!"

"Pull over," Erin said compassionately. "I'm sure he just wants to give you one final hug goodbye."

"This is so embarrassing," I complained. "It's time to let me go! Cut the cord, already! I'm twenty-three years old, for crying out loud!"

Nevertheless, I stopped and rolled down my window, expecting an emotional plea to be careful or for him to reminisce about how he fainted in the hospital delivery room upon learning that he was having a boy. That's not what I got.

"Greg, you knucklehead!" he yelled. "Don't you see what's still parked in front of the house?"

I looked carefully in the mirror, and sure enough, there sat my car. Somehow, the car must have fallen off the hitch when I popped the clutch. It turned out that I'd forgotten to insert the safety pin on the trailer ball.

"So, that's what that's for!" I jokingly exclaimed after realizing my mistake.

Erin thought it was "adorable" that I didn't think to check the safety pin, and she laughed hysterically.

I backed up the truck, reattached my car, and fastened the safety pin. Unfortunately, my mistake had cost us about forty-five minutes. I figured we could still make Denver by late night—but by four o'clock that afternoon, I was bone tired.

"Honey, you have to drive," I said to Erin. "I'm exhausted."

"You have to be kidding," she replied. "There's no *way* I'm driving this . . . semi-truck!"

I'd hoped for a different response, but her fear of driving the "tiny" U-Haul truck cracked me up. *She's afraid to drive . . . how cute*, I thought.

Besides, I just wanted to be together on our first grand adventure as an engaged couple.

So with no other options open to me, I explained my need for something to keep me awake. I figured that since Erin was a nurse, I was speaking to the right person.

"That's simple," she declared. "Pull in to that truck stop."

When I did, she climbed out of the truck, and a few minutes later she returned with a bag full of energy products like vitamin B-12, caffeine powder, NoDoz pills, Jolt Cola—anything with high levels of caffeine.

"Are you sure I can take all of this stuff together?" I asked, a little concerned.

"Sure," she replied. "Trust me." Then I heard her mumble under her breath, "At least, I think it's all right."

I quickly doused my system with torrents of caffeine, and the moment it hit, I felt as if I could drive 8,500 miles rather than a mere 850. I gave Erin a big toothy grin, leaned over, and shouted, "How far is Canada?"

We drove on, laughing, talking, and watching the scenery fly by. We talked about goals and aspirations that we wanted to accomplish together that would take us the next fifty years to achieve. Our fairy tale was starting off with a bang!

But by one o'clock in the morning, the caffeine had worn off and the sugar high was long gone, and I couldn't drive another mile.

"If we don't find a place to stop immediately," I whined, "I'm going to literally crash and burn—I'm going to kill us."

We had nearly reached Colorado Springs, and it seemed as good a place as any to stop. But we immediately ran into a big problem. Parents' Weekend at the Air Force Academy had arrived, and every room in every hotel and motel in the city had been taken. This must have been how Mary and Joseph felt stumbling into Bethlehem.

We searched for a frustrating hour before someone suggested a motel downtown. *Horse stable or not*, I thought, *here we come!*

When we arrived at the U-shaped, rundown motel (and calling it a *motel* is generous) with an office shack in the middle, I wheeled our truck around the whole complex. By then my exhaustion had nearly given way to delirium.

"I need two rooms," I sleepily told the office manager.

"Sorry, I have only one," he answered.

Of course! I thought.

"Does it have two beds?" I asked.

"No, just one," he quickly answered while looking confused. "All we got are the queen beds with the coin-operated massage feature."

Oh, all right, I thought. *I guess I'll sleep on the floor. No big deal. At least we'll have two pillows.*

"I'll take it," I replied wearily.

"How many hours would you like the room for?" he asked.

What a bizarre question. I consulted my watch. It was 2:35 a.m. If we could sleep for five hours, we would still make Denver by nine o'clock in the morning.

"I need the room for five hours," I said.

"Way to *go*, buddy!" he snorted.

Completely oblivious to his meaning, I replied innocently, "Most of the time," I shrugged my shoulders, "I rent a room *all* night."

The man doubled over with laughter and gave me a high five as he handed me a sheet set and towels.

Odd, I thought, as I turned away from the counter.

"This is a really strange place," I told Erin, "but it's our only option. I'll sleep on the floor. Let's call our parents to let them know."

But the phones wouldn't work. The last straw! *Forget it,* I thought, and took my place on the cold, gross red shag carpet.

The next morning, I woke up stiff from a terrible night's sleep. I hobbled over to the office and handed the keys, sheets, and towels to the same man who had checked us in the night before. He seemed terribly upset.

"Everything okay?" I asked.

"None of the phones work," he moaned. "I can't figure out why. This is going to cost me *money!*"

"Tell me about it," I replied. "My fiancée and I tried to call our parents last night to let them know what happened. We didn't want anyone to wonder why we stayed in the same room, so we . . ."

My voice trailed off when it became clear he had zero interest in my story.

I left to buy Erin a Diet Coke and myself a Mountain Dew out of the vending machine. Thanks to Erin I was in the midst of a wicked caffeine withdrawal! However, trying to feed a wrinkled dollar bill into the payment slot, I noticed a severed cable lying on the ground. *That's weird*, I thought.

As I walked around the complex, every few feet I noticed another severed cable lying on the pavement—until I reached my U-Haul truck. There, six inches from the front of my vehicle, hung one last cable still in place. And then it hit me: I had clipped all the phone lines when I drove around the facility the night before!

I ran into our room, yelling, "Erin! Get into the truck *now!* We have to get out of here!"

Erin, of course, wondered if I had just robbed the manager. When she heard the real story, she rightly insisted that we pay for the damage. After shelling out cash for the damaged phone lines and the hourly rate, I realized that disgusting little room with red shag carpet and the massage bed ended up costing me more than the presidential suite in a pricey hotel!

Still, we laughed all the way from Colorado Springs to Denver and dreamed about our future together. Why? Because when you are at the front end of your relationship and wildly in love, major blunders like knocking your car off the trailer, over-dosing your fiancé on caffeine, and destroying a seedy motel's phone system are hilarious.

In the beginning of a marriage, the whole world seems enchanting. Life is viewed through rose-colored glasses. Personality quirks seem adorable. Time together is at the top of the to-do list. You talk—at a deep emotional level. You listen. You pay attention. You date. You woo. You connect. You laugh and have fun. You agree on what to watch. You have shared interests. Sex is passionate. You kiss before parting ways and welcome each other home with excitement. Conflicts are resolved quickly. Mistakes get U-Haul–sized truckloads of grace and forgiveness. You pray together. You dream about the future. You see the very best in each other. You're best friends—soulmates. It's why you got married.

That's almost always how it is at the beginning of marriage. But, then, something goes wrong—subtly, almost imperceptibly wrong. And one day you wake up and realize that you're in love with a stranger.

The Little Foxes

Thousands of years ago, King Solomon's bride-to-be (the Shulammite maiden) warned of little foxes that can destroy the vineyards of love. "Catch all the foxes, those little foxes, before they ruin the vineyard of love, for the grapevines are blossoming!" (Song of Solomon 2:15, NLT). In Solomon's day, a fox was a troublesome little creature that would sneak into the vineyards, gnaw on leaves, break branches, eat the grapes, and dig deep holes to nibble at the roots—ultimately spoiling the vines.

But notice the Shulammite maiden uses the phrase "little foxes." She is distinguishing between the big threats of her time—wild beasts like boars and lions—and the small, mischievous creatures that could slyly damage their budding relationship. She's wisely encouraging her husband-to-be to take preventive action to protect their love from little threats that could wreak havoc on their future relationship. In essence she's saying, "Protect us by removing whatever might harm our marriage—especially the small things that will spoil our growing roots!"

I (Greg) wish I'd heeded the Shulammite maiden's warning. Erin was right that day when she broke down crying about the state of our marriage. Little foxes had invaded our relationship. We had subtly drifted apart over the years—I just wasn't paying attention. My obliviousness resulted from being focused on guarding our marriage from the big issues—infidelity, pornography, abuse, addictions, etc. I was determined that these "wild beasts" would never destroy our vineyard. I was absorbed with the big threats—like a sentry standing at the gate with a huge pair of binoculars scanning the horizon looking for the obvious dangers. And while I stood safeguarding, I missed the little foxes that had dug under the gate and snuck into our vineyard—robbing our relationship of its delicious fruit and gnawing at our roots. But in our case, the mischievous little creatures didn't destroy our love; they morphed us from soulmates into roommates.

What are these little foxes that can destroy a marriage or create married roommates?

Researchers have been curious about this question as well. Every day millions of internet users ask Google life's most difficult questions. One of the most common Google queries is "Why do relationships end?"[1] Author Nell Frizzell wrote the following:

> A wise man once told me that nobody breaks up over adultery, but over the way you talk at dinner . . . the small daily incivilities, the apologies unspoken, the kisses that go unkissed, the meals that pass in silence, the money that is wasted—these lay the groundwork for the big things to erupt. Infidelity happens, perhaps, when one partner or the other is looking to plug a hole—not just a physical one but an emotional one, a personal one, a psychological one laid bare by months and years of ugly lampshades, boring weekends, and lukewarm pasta bakes. Separation is perhaps the inevitable endpoint of eating at different times, sleeping on the sofa because you got home late, choosing to go on holiday with someone else, watching different things on your phones instead of going to the cinema and making plans in which the other is not included.[2]

Social scientists have diligently searched for answers to this same question and have made some astonishing discoveries. In the United States, researchers estimate that 40 to 50 percent of all first marriages and 60 percent of second marriages will end in divorce.[3] Why? Several major research projects have focused on the specific reasons people give for their divorces:

- A 2003 study found that "growing apart" was fifth behind infidelity, incompatibility, drinking or drug use, and physical or mental abuse for why people divorced.[4]

- In 2004, AARP surveyed older adults (aged 40 and up) and reported abuse, differing values and lifestyles, cheating, and "simply falling out of love/no obvious problems" as the top four reasons for divorce.[5]

- In 2006, a study out of the Netherlands found that the third main reason that females gave for divorce was "growing apart" (behind not enough attention and not able to talk). The men listed "growing apart" as the top reason for divorce.[6]

- In a study published in 2012, researchers found the two most common reasons for divorcing were "growing apart" and "not being able to talk together."[7]

- According to the more than 800,000 individuals who have completed the *Focus on Marriage* assessment, the top five marriage struggles are: (1) sex, (2) conflict, (3) communication, (4) shared responsibility, and (5) time together. Interestingly enough, these struggles are how roommate marriages are described: sexless marriage, not working through conflicts, no meaningful communication, household chores that aren't divided equally, and busyness and routine replacing quality time together (visit www.FocusontheFamily.com/marriageassessment to take our free marriage assessment).

Growing apart, not being able to talk together, not enough attention, falling out of love, no obvious problems—these are all different ways to say these couples ended up as married roommates. As a younger husband, I was living out these research findings and our marriage was at a point of crisis. I didn't want to exist like roommates with Erin, or worse yet, end up as another divorce statistic.

The start of our marriage revitalization began by understanding what had gone wrong in our relationship—how our deep love (like we had on that crazy drive to Denver) had morphed into gentle neglect, silent routines, and polite indifference. How did we go from soulmates to roommates?

From Lovers to Roomies

Certainly big issues such as abuse, infidelity, pornography, and addictions wreak havoc in a marriage. We're not trying to minimize their destructive impact. If your marriage has been affected by one of these "wild beasts," you need to get professional help immediately. Focus on the Family has an amazing intensive counseling program called *Hope Restored* for couples in crisis. It has an 80 percent success rate for couples on the brink of divorce (visit www.HopeRestored.com for more information). However, we can't overlook that "growing apart" consistently shows up as a main reason cited for divorce.

For couples who feel like married roommates, it's a slow fade. People don't fall in love, get married, and then intentionally disconnect. It usually takes years for the passion, intimacy, and connection within a marriage to deteriorate. Left unnoticed, soulmates slowly morph into roommates. Passion turns into mundane routine. Intimacy turns into disinterest. Connection changes to icy distance. Sex is traded for sleep. Enjoyment and fun mutate into boredom. Meaningful conversation is replaced by business meetings. Peace becomes tension. Shared dreams vanish.

While roommates do all the hard work associated with being married, very few experience the amazing benefits of being married. Compared to singles, married couples live longer, are wealthier, enjoy certain tax deductions, and have better health insurance coverage and retirement benefits.

As romantic as a good tax break sounds, these advantages would never inspire someone to get down on bended knee and beseech their beloved to spend a lifetime together. I didn't ask Erin to marry me for better insurance coverage and tax advantages (although the wealthier part sounds intriguing). I wanted to spend life with my best friend and experience passion, romance, sex, meaningful conversation, deep connection, encouragement, shared dreams, laughter, praying together, flirting, peace, pursuing Christ together, and oneness. The anticipation of sharing these wonderful experiences is what compelled us into marriage. Sadly, roommate marriages miss out on these thrilling benefits.

The phrase "married roommates" can look different depending on the couple. We have done extensive research to understand the subtle differences to help you pinpoint what is really going on in your relationship and to identify roommate-like behaviors—the little foxes—that find their way into the vineyard of love. We have isolated eleven behaviors that slowly morph couples from soulmates to roommates. For you, there might be one glaring reason or it may be a combination of multiple behaviors that have ensnared your marriage. Feeling like roommates is on a continuum; it's not a yes or no question. And growing apart is life-stage dependent. A couple with young children will experience this differently than a couple with no children. You might go through a season of disconnection. Or you may feel that things are going pretty well now, but there might be some behaviors that could create problems down the road. Wherever you are today, understanding the little foxes is critical to having the marriage you long for.

As you read through the following descriptions, use the following scale to establish the extent that you relate to each of the eleven issues and how it currently impacts your marriage.

1—I don't relate *at all*
2—I relate *slightly*
3—I relate *moderately*
4—I relate *very much*
5—I relate *completely*

Eleven characteristics of married roommates:

1. **Exhausted**: You are sleep-deprived, tired, or burned-out. The cause of your fatigue is often beyond your control and based on your circumstances or season of life. Realities such as raising kids, starting a new job or business, caring for an aging parent, a medical illness, or dealing with a special needs child leave you feeling exhausted. As a result, you are more sensitive, more easily offended, more confrontational, and more likely to say things you regret. You are less likely to have the energy to invest in your spouse or marriage.

Circle the number that best describes the extent to which this issue is true in your marriage right now.

1 – 2 – 3 – 4 – 5

2. **Busy**: You feel like two ships passing in the night. It's easy to feel disconnected when priorities get misaligned and schedules are out-of-sync because the focus is on work, kids, housework, yard work, friends, hobbies, bills, church, and so on. Your hectic schedules and demanding responsibilities leave little time for each other. Spending quality time together has fallen to the bottom of your to-do list.

1 – 2 – 3 – 4 – 5

3. **Pragmatic**: You have a business-like relationship as you do life together. Most of your communication is around "administrating" your marriage—talking about to-do lists, schedules, kids, finances, and so on. Your communication seems to have been relegated to short directives and curt responses. This leaves hardly

any time for meaningful conversation where you talk about your inner life—emotions, needs, hopes, fears, and dreams.

1 – 2 – 3 – 4 – 5

4. **Gentle Neglect:** You or your marriage is constantly taking a back burner to jobs, kids, friends, housework, and hobbies. You feel ignored. You don't feel like a priority. Television, social media, kids, work, sports, and hobbies monopolize your evenings or weekend time. When you are together, your spouse is constantly checking his or her phone for texts, news, social media, or games. You feel invisible.

1 – 2 – 3 – 4 – 5

5. **Complacent:** Many people work hard to "win" their spouse and then over time they become comfortable. The initial excitement associated with getting to know a person, growing in intimacy, and trying new things as a couple can disappear as the two people settle into a routine. It's not that we lose interest in our spouse. We become comfortable. We don't feel like we need to make much of an effort. The romantic spark fades or is replaced by the mundane. The marriage feels predictable—boring even.

1 – 2 – 3 – 4 – 5

6. **Spiritually Distant:** You rarely pray together, seldom talk about spiritual matters, hardly ever attend church together, and don't have Christian friends that you hang out with together at church or in a small fellowship group. You don't feel "equally yoked." The lack of spiritual intimacy has created distance in

your marriage and you don't feel like you connect at a deep spiritual level—soul to soul.

1 – 2 – 3 – 4 – 5

7. **Conflict Avoidance**: You or your spouse evade difficult conversations, sweep negative issues under the rug, or rarely bring an argument to resolution in a way that both people feel good about. When we avoid conflict, problems don't get resolved and these small frustrations grow into big issues down the road. Avoidance decreases intimacy and creates distance because problems aren't being addressed and resolved. Over time, spouses stop trying to work things out and deal with the relationship problems individually. Ultimately, the strategy of avoiding problems blows up and spouses feel resentful and alone.

1 – 2 – 3 – 4 – 5

8. **Sexless**: Sex is an important part of a marriage. And yet, researchers estimate that 15 to 20 percent of US couples haven't had sex in the past 12 months.[8] In a sexless marriage, sex becomes routine, dutiful, infrequent, or nonexistent. Sex only happens if it's on the calendar. Romance has faded, affection is absent, and foreplay is a distant memory. Certainly there is a natural ebb and flow of a sexual relationship in marriage depending on what season of life you're in or the circumstances you're facing. However, when we deprioritize sex, passion is replaced by boring routine, duty, or avoidance. Ultimately, spouses feel rejected, lonely, and resentful—susceptible to finding emotional and physical connection outside the marriage.

1 – 2 – 3 – 4 – 5

9. **Disengaged:** Your marriage feels like each individual is going in separate directions. It seems like the kids are about the only thing you have in common. Certainly couples shouldn't be together 24-7—it's healthy to have alone time away from each other. We're not talking about good self-care here. Instead, in this roommate state, most of your activities are done separately and you hardly see each other when at home. You have separate bedtimes, maintain separate checking accounts, sleep in separate rooms, take separate vacations, and have separate hobbies—you feel like you're leading parallel lives. Over time, disengaged couples have nothing in common and simply exist in proximity to each other.

1 – 2 – 3 – 4 – 5

10. **Unsafe:** We live in a harsh world. Satan—our sworn enemy—is like a lion, constantly on the prowl, ready to strike. Work is stressful. Children are a handful. Friends disappoint. News is depressing. Social media makes us feel jealous and like we don't measure up. Road rage is widespread. Sexual harassment is our country's dirty little secret. Racial tensions still exist. Political fighting is despicable. Terrorism is here to stay. Internet trolls are constantly spewing hatred. At the same time, our homes should be sanctuaries from this disheartening chaos. However, for many couples, their relationship is not a refuge. The marriage feels tense or strained. Instead of feeling relaxed, you feel like you're walking on eggshells and feel apprehensive around your spouse. Instead of peace, anger is constantly rearing its ugly head. Instead of acceptance, you feel relentlessly nit-picked and you don't feel free to be yourself. When you don't feel safe, over time individuals will disconnect and hearts will eventually harden—the deathblow for a marriage.

1 – 2 – 3 – 4 – 5

11. **Visionless**: Most dating and engaged couples dream wildly of what their life will look like together. But then life gets busy. Juggling a marriage, running a household, balancing careers, raising children, and a thousand other challenges, cause big dreams to be set aside. Thus, you don't share a clear dream for the life you're building together. You don't have a vision of how you will use your "oneness" to serve God and bless others.

1 – 2 – 3 – 4 – 5

How did you rate each issue? Was there one main struggle or have several issues combined to leave you feeling like roommates? Perhaps there are a few behaviors that are taking place that you want to guard against. Awareness and insight are important first steps to reconnecting. This information is vital to reverse a trend or to prevent these issues from taking root in your marriage.

Looking back, we would have strongly connected with several of these roommate behaviors. We were exhausted from finishing graduate school, parenting three young children, and starting careers as marriage counselors (we know . . . the irony). We were empty and constantly served each other relational leftovers. Our demanding responsibilities left little time for each other, and spending quality time stopped being a priority. What little time we spent in actual conversation defaulted to figuring out how to manage our hectic schedules or dealing with mounting problems. The final straw, however, was gentle neglect.

I (Greg) remember avoiding alone time with Erin because I was certain we'd talk about either our boring schedules and to-do lists or we'd argue about something trivial. Also, I poorly handled my own stress by checking out emotionally and escaping into my "man cave" to watch television. Poorly managing my stress and exhaustion left Erin feeling abandoned in our marriage. As a result of these roommate-like behaviors, we both began to question our love for each other. We put more emphasis on raising our children and less priority on our marriage. It was a vicious cycle. I didn't realize it at the time, but we were experiencing the exact reasons people gave for getting a divorce: growing apart, not being able to talk together, not enough attention, falling out of love with no obvious problems. These little foxes had ravaged our vineyard of love, and our marriage was slowly fading into extinction. When you behave like roommates, the real dangers are these little foxes.

For so many couples, their marriages started out great and remained that way for several years. And then the slow fade was set in motion by the little foxes of exhaustion, busyness, complacency, ignored problems, boredom, routine, fading passion, nonexistent sex, different interests, and different priorities. Over time, neglect weakened their relationship.

But here is the silent killer of the marriage. When spouses feel ignored or disconnected, over time they start to deal with their problems apart from each another. Emotional closeness fades into indifference or resentment. As they get good at working out their issues alone, they start leading parallel lives. They coexist, but they begin to separate emotionally, spiritually, and physically. And when the couple starts to lead fully parallel lives, isolation and loneliness follow close behind. Couples slowly lose interest in each other and grow apart with no obvious problems until they wake up one day feeling emotionally dead, wondering, "Where did our love go?"

Roommate marriages rarely survive long-term. Beyond the misery of a slow fade, the final deathblow is loneliness.

Loneliness is in stark contrast to God's design for marriage. It was a powerful moment in the creation story when God declared that it wasn't good for man to be alone (Genesis 2:18) and then promptly created a lifelong soulmate for Adam—not a playmate or companion. We love how Eugene H. Peterson captures the first wedding in Genesis 2:23-25:

The Man said, "Finally! Bone of my bone, flesh of my flesh! Name her Woman for she was made from Man." Therefore a man leaves his father and mother and embraces his wife. They become one flesh. The two of them, the Man and his Wife, were naked, but they felt no shame (MSG).

God created us as relational beings. We long for connection and intimacy—to know and be known by another at the deepest level. Feeling isolated and alone goes against our heart's desire. It's like sucking the air out from around us. Such a relationship will not last. As loneliness spreads, divorce enters the picture.

Maybe you haven't reached a crisis point in your marriage but you sense the disconnection, tension, and loneliness that comes from living with roommate-like behaviors. Wherever you find yourself today, you can rediscover your soulmate and revive your marriage! And you'll find the roadmap within the pages of this book.

Before we jump into the reconnect plan, we want to say a word about the concept of soulmates. When we use the word *soulmate*, we're not talking about the magical concept that implies God created one special person just for you—one true love. Who can forget the famous line from the movie *Jerry Maguire*, "You complete me." Our culture describes a soulmate as your heart's other half—the person to whom you're bound by destiny to share your life with. That one person who completes you and "makes you feel entirely whole, healed and intact—like no piece is missing from the puzzle."[9] We do not believe that there is one true love and you won't be complete until you find that person. God completes you. Christ is your true source of fulfillment. Our idea of a soulmate is a spouse with whom you enter into a covenant relationship with God for a lifetime and regularly experience the deepest levels of connection and intimacy. This is our idea of being married to your best friend—your soulmate (or *sole* mate).

So let's get started catching those little foxes before they ruin the vineyard of your love!

CHAPTER 2

Fully Alive

Self care is never a selfish act—it is simply good stewardship of the only gift I have, the gift I was put on earth to offer others.

PARKER PALMER

Roommates are exhausted and have nothing to give; soulmates give regularly out of an abundantly full heart.

LIFE FEELS FASTER, BUSIER, and more hectic. It's as if something or *someone* is conspiring to keep us exhausted and damage our marriages one frenzied moment at a time. It reminds us of a story written by Geraldine Harris and Kristen Maddox about Satan's reworked plan to "*steal, kill, and destroy.*"

Satan called a worldwide convention. In his opening address to his demons, he said, "We can't keep the Christians from going to church. We can't keep them from reading their Bibles and knowing the truth. We can't even keep them from biblical values. But we can do something else. We can keep them from forming an intimate, continual experience with Christ.

"If they gain that connection with Jesus, our power over them is broken. So let them go to church, let them have their Christian lifestyles, but steal their time so they can't gain that experience with Jesus Christ.

"This is what I want you to do. Distract them from gaining hold of their Savior and maintaining that vital connection throughout their day."

"How shall we do this?" asked his demons.

"Keep them busy with the nonessentials of life and invest unnumbered schemes to occupy their minds," he answered.

"Tempt them to spend, spend, spend, then borrow, borrow, borrow. Convince them to work six or seven days a week, 10–12 hours a day, so they can afford their lifestyles. Keep them from spending time with their spouse and children. As their families fragment, soon their homes will offer no escape from the pressures of work.

"Overstimulate their minds so they cannot hear that still small voice. Entice them to keep the TV, computers, tablets, smartphones and video games going constantly in their homes. Pound their minds with social media and news 24 hours a day. Invade their driving moments with endless choices of music, sports and talk radio. Flood their mailboxes and email with junk, sweepstakes, and every kind of newsletter and promotion.

"Even in their recreation, let them be excessive. Have them return from their holidays exhausted, disquieted, and unprepared for the coming week. And when they gather for spiritual fellowship, involve them in gossip and small talk so they leave with souls unfulfilled.

"Let them be involved in evangelism. But crowd their lives with so many good causes that they have no time to seek power from Christ. Soon they will be working in their own strength, sacrificing their health, and family unity for the good of the cause."

It was quite a convention. And the demons went eagerly to their assignments.[1]

The "Spin Class" of Life

Has Satan's plan worked? It sure seems effective. We live in a fast-paced, busy culture. We have full plates overflowing with good things: jobs, children, kid activities, household responsibilities, hobbies, leisure activities, church, community service, outreach projects, small-group fellowship, Bible studies, extended family, and friends. But we are left breathless—feeling overworked and exhausted.

We have an enemy radically devoted to keeping us overwhelmed, and he fools us into staying busy doing "good things." When we lament about our hurried life, our culture beats us up by sending a clear message: "Don't be such a whiner. You made these choices. So, buck up, buttercup, and push on." For many, we're afraid of failing or that people will think we're weak or that we can't cope. So we've become our own harshest critic and believe that we just need to "suck it up." Instead of learning how to take care of our weary souls, most of us watched our parents exist in this same tired and overloaded life. So we trudge on like the living dead.

But this "suck it up" strategy isn't working. Ignoring our exhausted hearts and bodies only makes things worse. We take fewer vacations, work longer hours, cobble together more jobs to make ends meet, and retire later. There are endless chores required to maintain a household and to raise our children. We want more stuff and go into debt for luxury items. As parents we want the very best for our children so we overdo sports, private lessons, parties, outings, and education. We spend countless hours stuck in traffic. We compete with friends and neighbors for the best looking lawn and the newest car. We double book appointments. We seem to be late for everything. We are connected to technology 24-7, which leaves us constantly "on call" and unable to get away from the drudgery. Social media breeds envy as "perfect" images of friends and family members endlessly parade across our screens. We know we should be connecting as a couple so we plan date nights and weekend getaways that never seem to materialize. We want it all. We expect it all. We want to be the perfect employee, boss, parent, spouse, son, daughter, friend, and Christian. But the high standards and striving are taking a toll on us physically and relationally. We are rushed and hurried—with little margin. We're burned out, stressed out, sick, tired, depressed, anxious, grumpy, resentful, and angry, and our relationships feel isolated, disconnected, and strained.

On the other hand, the cause of your exhaustion might be beyond your control or based on your particular circumstances or season of life. Realities such as raising young kids, starting a new job or business, caring for an aging parent, a medical illness, or dealing with a child with special needs leave you feeling physically worn-out and emotionally drained.

Think about this past week. Did your schedule feel hectic? Did you feel rushed? Do you remember feeling overcommitted—that your plate was overflowing? Are you tired, exhausted, or sleep-deprived? But here's the real question you need to answer: Is this strategy working?

There is a high cost for the fast pace we are living. Overloaded schedules lead to hectic interactions that lead to exhausted people who are empty. Combining two smaller symbols forms the Chinese symbol for "busyness." One symbol is for "heart" and the other symbol is for "killing." Busyness can kill your heart by limiting your connection to God (the source of life) and time with your spouse and family. With an empty and deadened heart, our relationships suffer because empty people have nothing to give. In the end, our spouse and children get relational leftovers, and relationships can't survive long on table scraps. So, what's the answer? Do we "suck it up" and squeeze out what little energy reserves we have left?

The key has everything to do with time—but we're not suggesting time *management*. We're not going to give a bunch of tips to better manage your time. We don't believe the answer is necessarily doing less. Our goal is to help you give more, not less—but from a place of abundance, not emptiness. It's about discovering a rhythm that keeps your body rested and your heart alive.

The Rhythm of Godly Self-Care

As a young boy, my (Greg's) mother made me play the piano. It was a painful part of my childhood. When my friends were outside playing after school, I was stuck practicing on an old rickety piano. Mrs. Johnson was a kind and patient woman who had to endure thirty minutes of me whining every Wednesday afternoon in the Smalley home. Aside from the trauma of missing precious playtime with my friends, about all I remember from Mrs. Johnson's lessons was her metronome—that pyramid-shaped wooden contraption with the long metal bar that swings back and forth and makes a clicking sound. I was certain her metronome was some medieval device used to hypnotize young boys into practicing the piano.

At the time, I had no idea that Mrs. Johnson's metronome was teaching me a powerful lesson well beyond the piano.

Musicians have used metronomes for centuries to help them develop a strong sense of rhythm and tempo. A metronome produces a steady beat that lets us know if we are slowing down or speeding up while practicing. Musicians are free to think about other things in music, such as phrasing and dynamics because the metronome keeps them in line.[2]

Mrs. Johnson was trying to teach me to play with the right pace—to know how fast or slow to play a song. She was using her metronome to force me to pay attention to *time*. In the same way, we need an "inner metronome" to pay attention to the time, rhythm, and pace of our lives. The enemy wants us to exist in a fast-paced, chaotic rhythm—he wants to run us ragged. But God designed us for a more restful and purposeful life. In his book *The Life You've Always Wanted*, John Ortberg recalls a time when he approached his mentor wanting to know how he could deepen his relationship with God. Ortberg's mentor replied, "You must ruthlessly eliminate hurry from your life."[3] What great advice. God didn't intend us to live exhausted, joyless, stressed out, depressed, worn down, overloaded, hurried, bitter, burned-out, resentful, and empty lives because it keeps us from living out His greatest commandments (to love

God and others) and ultimately hinders our marriages as we become weary roommates.

The marriage you're longing for requires wholehearted engagement on the part of the individuals. Love requires an open and abundantly full heart. Connection requires endurance. Passion requires energy. Intimacy requires attentiveness. Fun and laughter require reserves. Grace requires persistence. Forgiveness requires strength. All these things are possible in marriage, but these things won't happen if your rhythm and pace is hurried, your body is exhausted, and your heart is empty.

Jesus talked about the importance of a wholehearted love when He was asked which of God's commandments was the greatest: "'And you shall love the Lord your God with all your heart and with all your soul and with all your mind and with all your strength.' The second is this: 'You shall love your neighbor as yourself.' There is no other commandment greater than these" (Mark 12:30-31). Simply put, *love* is our mandate. God wants us to love Him and others wholeheartedly—with all of our heart, soul, mind, and strength. Jesus went on to clarify that out of everything that we could do, loving others is the best proof that we are Christ-followers (John 13:34-35). It stands to reason, then, that a bunch of empty and exhausted people can't love as God has instructed. At some point our Christian culture has rewritten the greatest commandments from loving God and others *as yourself* to loving God and others *instead of yourself*. But we can't give what we don't have.

This is why Satan is so ruthlessly committed to your being empty and exhausted. He wants to steal your time by keeping you busy. He wants to kill your heart by keeping you overwhelmed. He wants to destroy your vital connection with God by keeping you preoccupied doing too many good things.

Jesus wants the exact opposite. It's why He implores us to understand why He came to this earth. "The thief comes only to steal and kill and destroy. I came that they may have life and have it abundantly" (John 10:10). Jesus doesn't just want to save us; He wants us to have a full and abundant life so that we can love God and others whole-heartedly. So the real question is who is winning the battle over your inner metronome—the enemy or Christ?

As is always the case, God has a wonderful solution. We think the solution requires that you discover the rhythm and pace of your inner metronome by answering two important questions: What brings you rest? What brings you life?

What Brings You Rest?

What do you do when you're tired? Drink a third cup of Death Wish Coffee, veg out in front of the TV, guzzle an energy drink, grab a quick nap in the carpool lane, or pound a bag of Doritos or something sweet? Unfortunately, these survival behaviors rarely rejuvenate us and most often do the exact opposite—leaving us jittery or feeling guilty about the extra calories.

So what gives you real rest?

Rest is when you "cease work or movement in order to relax, refresh oneself, or recover strength."[4] Rest is meant to "recharge" you and help you recover strength. But rest is often misunderstood. It's seen as idleness and laziness—the opposite of productivity! As if we've been "turned off" (dead), versus being "turned on" (alive). And no one wants to be viewed as unproductive or dead. Rest is also seen as boring or the enemy of fun and life. Some even view rest as a form of spiritual deficiency by misapplying King Solomon's statement that "idle hands are the devil's workshop" (Proverbs 16:27, TLB). But rest is not laziness. Consider this explanation from *Psychology Today*:

> What rest is: regeneration, the way your body lives, thrives,
> and survives, using the information it receives and creates. Stop
> sleep and you can die. Short shrift sleep and you wreck your
> ability to learn and remember, increase your chance of stroke

and heart attack, set yourself up for colds, mess up your skin and set yourself to gain weight, quickly and reliably.

And that's just a passive form of rest, sleep.

Because there's far more—the active forms of rest you consciously control that reactivate your own regeneration. There's physical rest, mental rest, social rest, spiritual rest, ways to renew you and restore you as your body rebuilds itself.[5]

Our fast-paced society regularly trades rest for overwork. This puts such a strain on our bodies. It doesn't matter if you sit at a desk or do manual labor; your body and mind need rest to recuperate. When we don't rest physically, mentally, emotionally, and spiritually, we run the risk of injury to our bodies and relationships. This is why God encourages us to rest throughout the Scriptures:

Be still, and know that I am God. (Psalm 46:10)

But they who wait for the LORD shall renew their strength; they shall mount up with wings like eagles; they shall run and not be weary; they shall walk and not faint. (Isaiah 40:31)

For whoever has entered God's rest has also rested from his works as God did from his. (Hebrews 4:10)

Jesus himself modeled rest—often withdrawing to the wilderness to be alone, sending crowds of people away so He could be alone with His friends, going to social events when He could have been "working," sleeping while everyone else was panicking, and once even hiding from His disciples. Jesus even called His disciples to rest. He said, "'Come away by yourselves to a desolate place and rest a while.' For many were coming and going, and they had no leisure even to eat" (Mark 6:31). Jesus was not selfish; He was simply doing what He needed to do to prevent exhaustion and emptiness.

God's formula is pretty simple: *Be still. Wait upon the Lord. Come and rest. Rest from your work as I've rested.* Simple, practical, and countercultural. Rest involves building breaks into our lives before we collapse and finding activities that rejuvenate us. Rest is not passive but active. Here are just a few activities to help you rest well and reenergize:

Spend time with God. Go on a spiritual retreat or find a special place you can go to be quiet before the Lord and listen to His still small voice. "Come to me, all you who labor and are heavy laden, and I will give you rest" (Matthew 11:28).

Meditate on God's Word. There is a big difference between memorizing Bible verses and writing God's Word on your heart. When you meditate on Scripture, you repeat it over and over until it's been etched on the tablet of your heart.

Get plenty of sleep. Most healthy adults need at least seven hours of sleep per night to function at their best.[6] And even better, sleep can improve your marriage. We know this sounds farfetched but researchers from the University of Berkeley, California, found that a good night's sleep makes you less selfish. They found that couples who sleep well worked better together at tasks, encouraged each other more, and were more likely to say "thank you." Couples who slept well also appreciated each other more and regularly showed gratitude.[7]

Engage your funny bone. Laughter has amazing physiological effects that help you rest and relax. When you bust up over something funny, your body releases a whole cocktail of feel-good neurochemicals.[8]

Listen to music. Putting on music—of any kind—can also recharge you.

Read your Bible or a book.

Relax in nature.

Take a break from social media.

Take a leisurely walk.

Have a spa day or do massage therapy.

Eat healthy foods. Your diet and nutrition choices can make your stress levels go up or down. Certain foods provide comfort and actually increase levels of hormones in the body that naturally fight stress. Other types of foods and beverages can reduce stress by lowering the levels of hormones that trigger it.[9]

Soak in the tub.

Participate in a relaxing hobby.

Limit your caffeine intake. Caffeine in coffee, tea, energy drinks, some sodas, and chocolate can cause you to feel wound up, which can make stressful situations seem more intense.

Complete a puzzle.

Paint a picture or use an adult coloring book.

Watch a favorite movie or TV program. However, don't just watch TV mindlessly without purpose.

Observe the Sabbath every week. Make Sundays (or Saturdays) your day of rest.

Take a nap.

Sleep in.

Turn off the electronics and take a technology and digital sabbatical.

Snuggle with a loved one or pet.

Participate in stretching exercises.

Play an instrument.

Walk the dog.

What about you? *What activities will you invest in that will give you rest?* Get busy resting!

The other part of godly self-care is to discover and regularly participate in experiences that bring you *life*.

What Brings You Life?

Rest is important to rejuvenate your weary bones. But godly self-care also requires that you discover what causes your heart to come alive. Rest is vital but not sufficient.

Discovering what brings you life is part of taking great care of yourself. Remember, the goal of godly self-care is to give from a place of abundance. You are blessed to be a blessing to others. Are you bearing fruit and allowing others to benefit from God's love abundantly filling you? We should be like the tree by the stream that the prophet Jeremiah spoke about: "He is like a tree planted by water, that sends out its roots by the stream, and does not fear when heat comes, for its leaves remain green, and is not anxious in the year of drought, for it does not cease to bear fruit" (Jeremiah 17:8). Godly self-care helps your roots spread out and reach deep into God's life-giving water. When you learn to find rest and find life, you are not bothered by the heat or worried by long months of drought—your heart stays full.

To love others from a place of abundance, it's imperative that you devote time and resources to what invigorates you, to what brings passion, hope, creativity, and joy to your life. Life-giving activities feel like

God's breath entering your body and your weary bones coming alive (Ezekiel 37:4-5). Rest recharges your body; life awakens your soul.

It's infectious to encounter someone with a heart that is fully alive. What inspires you? What desires are locked deep inside you? What sets your soul on fire? What makes you come alive? What do you enjoy doing? What are you dreaming about accomplishing? What ignites you with passion?

We're not talking about activities that help you escape or distract you. The pursuit of money, education, a big house, or an expensive car can provide temporary happiness but will never keep your heart alive long-term. *Stuff* doesn't result in pure joy or cause your heart to come alive. Happiness is based on external circumstances and is temporary. Joy comes from within and can last much longer. God wants your heart abundantly full of traits such as love, joy, grace, peace, hope, patience, kindness, goodness, faithfulness, and gentleness. He wants these eternal qualities to overflow in you so you can bless others.

My (Erin) parents often told me that they didn't care what I did for a career. They just wanted me to choose something that I enjoyed since I would most likely be doing it for the next thirty to forty years. I knew from a young age that I wanted to be a labor and delivery nurse, and that's exactly what I became.

I will never forget the day I walked into my assigned room at work to be greeted by the sweetest expectant couple I'd ever met. As we began chatting, I soon learned that I had a connection with this couple—the husband had been Greg's high school football coach! What are the chances? The delivery was one I will always remember, not because of the shared connection, but the passion we all shared in reaching the finish line as well as avoiding a C-section. And with the Lord's help—it happened! Just a few months ago, I received a Facebook message from Lynn, telling me that her ten-pound baby girl was now getting married. And we reflected back and forth via Messenger, remembering the sweet moments we shared that day in the delivery room. Oh, the memories and the warmth that floods me thinking of how blessed I was to serve God in a field I not only loved, but also was passionate about!

For me (Greg), trout fishing in the mountains of Colorado brings me life. Standing in the middle of a cascading stream surrounded by pine trees and God's beauty ignites joy and passion within me. But fishing doesn't bring me rest. I'm usually worn out after a day of wading through a rushing river, and yet my heart has come alive. Erin and I recently spoke at a weekend marriage seminar. As we were flying home, I was exhausted. As an introvert, I love doing marriage events with my wife (this also brings me life), but after speaking and being around people for two days, I desperately needed a break. As soon as I boarded the plane, I put on my noise-canceling headphones, closed my eyes, and listened to my favorite music. Honestly, after a two-hour flight, I felt so rested because praise and worship music gives me true rest. However, I also needed something to bring me back to life. The next morning, I got up at five a.m. and drove two hours into the mountains and spent the day hiking at around 12,000 feet so I could fish in a mountain lake. I was in heaven! Although my body was tired from the long hike, my heart was alive and abundantly full.

We have asked thousands of people to share what experiences bring them life. The following list is intended to "prime the pump" and help you clarify what will ignite passion in your heart and help you stay abundantly full of joy. Also look at the earlier list of activities that bring rest. Some of those will apply here (such as spending time with God), so we won't mention them here.

Spend time with family.
Serve others.
Invest time in a hobby.
Have a coffee date with a close friend.
Exercise or work out.
Mentor a troubled teen or underprivileged youth.
Go on a mission trip.

Travel or go on vacation.

Conquer a fear. Take a risk and try a new activity—something out of the ordinary that pushes you out of your comfort zone.

Take a class or learn something new.

Learn a foreign language.

Teach a class.

Start your own business.

Regularly attend a Bible study class.

Go on an adventure to a museum, historical site, concert, play, etc.

Try creative writing or blogging about a topic you care about.

What about you? What activities will you invest in that will fill your heart to the measure of all the fullness of God?

We have full plates overflowing with good things. Again, this state of busyness leads to hectic interactions that lead to exhausted people who are empty and have deadened hearts. Ultimately we hurt and our relationships suffer because empty people have nothing to give.

This is exactly opposite of God's plan for us to love Him and others wholeheartedly and abundantly. The world needs people who are well-rested and alive!

Roommates are exhausted and have nothing to give;

soulmates give regularly out of an abundantly full heart.

CHAPTER 3

From Busyness to Connection

There is beauty and adventure in the commonplace
for those with eyes to see beyond.

JONATHAN LOCKWOOD HUIE

Roommates don't have time for each other;

soulmates use simple, everyday moments to stay connected.

WE LOVE SUSHI. Going out for sushi is one of our favorite date night activities. Several years ago a new sushi restaurant opened up close to our house. We were thrilled at the prospect of eating sushi without having to drive far—neighborhood sushi seemed like a dream come true.

As if it couldn't get any better, during our first visit we were greeted by the four most delightful words in the food industry: "All You Can Eat." Unlimited sushi at the edge of our neighborhood; it was like we'd died and gone to heaven. We're convinced the Wedding Feast of the Lamb in the book of Revelation will feature all-you-can-eat sushi!

We're not going to lie; we pounded sushi that night. The choices seemed endless, the quality was excellent, and the food was delicious. Every time our server walked by we ordered another round. It was like we'd discovered our own conveyor-belt sushi restaurant. We were having the best date night ever!

However, competitive food eaters we are not. We massively over-estimated our ability to consume sushi rolls. In the end, we were left with one large overflowing plate of sushi. No worries, we thought. We'll take it home and have lunch for the next several days—a true blessing in disguise!

When we asked our server for a to-go container, we were quickly informed (*shamed* was more like it) that leftovers couldn't be taken out of the restaurant. Worse yet, she pointed to the fine print on the menu explaining that we would be charged for any uneaten food. What? We were going to have to pay for our table scraps! I (Greg) quickly attempted to play the victim card and explained that because of my poor vision I didn't see the microscopic words, but to no avail. Our sushi Shangri-La instantly turned from the feast of the lamb to the feast of the losers. How hadn't we noticed this warning? Could it have been the seductive call of the sushi siren, urging us to eat more and more? Regardless, there we were holding a massive food bill from an overflowing plate of uneaten sushi.

What to do? Running seemed dishonest. Arguing with a sushi chef holding a very sharp Samurai sword-like knife seemed dangerous. Faking a heart attack seemed even more expensive. We'd already played the ignorance card. So, we were left with one viable option: finish eating the remaining rolls!

Already close to being in a food coma, we attempted to wolf down the remaining sushi. But with only a few pieces left, we tapped out. We were finished. We couldn't eat another bite. And we paid the price physically and financially!

That sushi place has become our favorite date night restaurant. We're much better now at regulating our food intake—although we laugh every time a server walks by carrying a massive wooden boat overflowing with sushi toward an unsuspecting patron with an appetite larger than their stomach capacity.

Busyness can feel like an overflowing plate of sushi after you've eaten your fill.

Overflowing Plates

Does it ever feel like "busy" has become the predictable answer we give when people ask how we're doing? Is this a badge of honor or a cry for help? A plate overflowing with 141 pieces of sushi often feels like the best description of our life together. If our life was a sushi-eating contest, we might be a record holder. And the irony is all these things are of our own doing. We built this life and have made these choices.

We're not complaining; we're just being honest about our schedules that feel overwhelming and to-do lists that never seem to end. The constant busyness controls us like the sushi server telling us we'll pay unless we keep eating. So bite after bite, we're consuming all that our life has to offer.

But not all couples choose their situation. For some, busyness is thrust upon them. There are special circumstances and unique seasons of life that require greater amounts of our time and attention beyond our control. But the net effect is the same whether busyness comes by our own choosing or through circumstances we can't control: *busyness makes it extremely challenging to find time, energy, and attention for our spouse.*

The busyness we're talking about in this chapter happens because it takes a lot to manage our lives together. Busy couples usually aren't intentionally rejecting their spouses or devaluing their relationships. They love their spouses and marriages. But over time they've created overflowing plates and can't figure out how to make room for each other.

What about you? Do you feel like two ships passing in the night? Does it seem like your schedules are totally out-of-sync? Has spending quality time together fallen to the bottom of your to-do list?

The problem with busyness is twofold.

First, busy people are spread thin and feel physically worn-out and emotionally depleted. This was our focus in the previous chapter.

Second, busy couples are disconnected. Take Nathan and Angela. They have been married for fifteen years and have a son in high school, a daughter in her last year of middle school, and a son in fourth grade.

They live just outside of a large city in the Midwest. Nathan manages an indoor sports complex, and Angela is a counselor for at-risk youth. Nathan volunteers on the audiovisual team at church, and Angela teaches a women's Bible study once a week. Nathan and Angela have been struggling lately to balance their work hours and kids' activities, and it often seems like they're just missing each other. Their high school son plays football in the fall, basketball in the winter, and runs track in the spring. The summer is filled with sports camps and tournaments. Their daughter loves dance and just made a dance squad in the city. Practices are four times a week with competitions on the weekends. The commute is thirty miles each way. Their youngest son has shown promise as a soccer player and recently was invited to play on an all-star traveling team. The great athletic opportunities for their kids require them to "divide and conquer"—with each parent chauffeuring a different child to activities during the week and going to separate games on the weekends so there's at least one parent at each game. Stress, lack of scheduling, and technology distractions add to a general sense of disconnection.

Imagine a typical evening at their home. Nathan has just rushed in the door from work. He hollers at his son because they are late for soccer practice. Angela is rushing to find their daughter and her car keys so she can take her to dance class. The couple troops the kids out the door and waves a wordless goodbye as they take turns backing out of the driveway. Two hours later, they all gather for a hasty meal of takeout. Nathan then disappears into the den to do paperwork, and Angela grabs her laptop and is soon immersed in preparing her Bible study lesson for tomorrow. Nathan ends up sound asleep long before Angela gets to their bedroom. She checks Facebook while Nathan snores away.

Nathan and Angela love each other but are so consumed by the concerns of each day that they miss many chances to connect on any meaningful level. Although they both want to spend more time together and as a family, they aren't sure how to make the needed changes.

The real threat for Nathan and Angela is letting their *connection* slip away. We've heard people suggest that the only difference between dating/cohabitating and being married is "legalized" sex, a public declaration of your love, and a state-issued marriage license. But this is far from the truth. Marriage creates emotional, health, and financial benefits, and married couples have the most satisfying sex on the planet! But we think the most unique difference between dating/cohabitation and marriage is the depth of connection and intimacy that results from a covenant relationship.

When the apostle Paul talks about marriage in Ephesians 5:31-32, he says, "'Therefore a man shall leave his father and mother and hold fast to his wife, and the two shall become one flesh.' This mystery is profound." The one-flesh bond between a husband and wife is a mysterious thing—very different from that of a dating or cohabitating couple. When two people make a lifelong commitment before God and to each other, a level of safety and security is created that can't be replicated in any other human relationship. When spouses trust the vows they made on their wedding day, there is a willingness to fully open their hearts and be completely known by their spouse at the deepest levels—spiritually, emotionally, mentally, and physically. There is a profound vulnerability and openness that is offered unlike anywhere else. We're not suggesting that every married couple reaches this depth of relationship or vulnerability—but the potential is there, and this is what's unique to marriage. This is the connection that we need to protect because it's what Satan is trying to disrupt and destroy in your marriage.

The lifeblood of marriage, the indispensable factor that gives something its strength and vitality, is connection and deep intimacy—knowing and being known at the deepest levels. Busyness hijacks connection and ushers in disengagement. This emotional and physical distance leads spouses to feel anxious and unsafe, and they slowly start to isolate from each other and withdraw from the relationship. It's what marriage expert Dr. John Gottman calls "the distance and isolation cascade."[1]

Love requires connection and time together. Many couples believe that their love will carry them through the busyness—that they'll reconnect when the kids are older or when things slow down. The problem is that you both are constantly changing, and many couples discover that after the kids are gone they are now living with a stranger. We can't put our relationship on hold in the midst of a busy season or when our plates are overflowing.

Marriage doesn't come with an autopilot or cruise control setting that allows us to simply push a button and attend to other obligations while our car drives down the road unattended—and still experience a thriving relationship. A marriage can't function like that. We must regularly invest in our marriage if we want to grow closer to each other.

Certainly you didn't stand before God and your friends on your wedding day and look deeply into your fiancé's eyes and imagine that words like *settling, maintaining, adequate,* and *good enough* would describe your marriage one day. So, how do you grow closer? How do you regularly invest in your marriage in the midst of busyness?

The Next Big Thing

When couples realize that busyness is killing their connection, they often cope with the inattention by focusing on the next "big thing." They believe that their relationship can exist from one big thing to the next—from date night to date night, from holiday to holiday, or from vacation to vacation. They want these encounters to be "perfect" and want their hopes of connection, intimacy, fun, and enjoyment to come true. However, they end up putting too much pressure on these experiences to compensate for months or years of neglect. This doesn't work. We encountered this truth the hard way—at least Greg did!

Family Camp. Those two words create hope that camping as a family will bring us closer together. At least that's what I (Greg) thought when I convinced my family to spend our Thanksgiving holiday in a rustic cabin on the beautiful shores of Green Lake, Wisconsin. It had been a busy year for the Smalley family. Our two oldest daughters were off to college, and Erin and I had been busy teaching marriage seminars around the country. Simply put, our family was exhausted and disconnected. But my hopes were high. Family Camp would change all of this. We would finally all be together, laughing, talking, playing, eating, resting, and most importantly—connecting!

We arrived late that first night and went straight to bed. The next morning, our entire family made the long, frigid walk to the dining hall—our family adventure was finally underway. Sadly, it didn't take more than 300 yards of family togetherness before our middle daughter, Murphy (eighteen at the time), and our son, Garrison (fifteen at the time), started bickering. Their squabble quickly went from minor irritation to all-out war. I tried to intervene as gently as I could. Well, to say that my peace negotiation failed would be an understatement. Murphy became so infuriated at Garrison that she yelled, "I'm done with this family," and ran off.

Murphy was a no-show for breakfast. When she finally reemerged at the cabin later that morning, I was furious. I gave her a stern piece of my mind, imploring her to act mature and get along with her brother! After my tirade, the entire family awkwardly stared off in silence.

"We will get along and we will have fun," I barked, and stormed out of the cabin.

Erin found me by the lake skipping rocks across the water. She asked me why I had gotten so angry. I had no idea! But I could feel the internal burn of frustration and sadness. The more we talked I finally had a realization. I had enormous expectations for our family time at camp. At some level, I was hoping that we would use this time to make up for any disconnection during the year. I quickly realized that I was putting an enormous amount of pressure on camp to revitalize our strained relationships.

What happened to me is what many couples experience, and it's why the "big things" such as date nights, vacations, holidays and family camps don't go as planned. The main issue is that our expectations often set us up for failure. We have to let go of the expectation that a few hours or days of being together can erase a year's (or decade's) worth of disconnection, neglect, conflict, and hurt. After recognizing this reality at family camp, I went back to our cabin and pulled the family together. I confessed my high expectations and the pressure I was feeling to have the perfect family reunion. I apologized for my angry outburst and committed to allowing family relationships to reconnect without my pressure and unrealistic expectations.

Did we end up having the magical family gathering that I'd originally envisioned? No. But it was good. We made some fun memories and got some rest. The best part for me was being freed from expectations that I didn't even know I had. I was able to fully invest in the imperfect experiences that unfolded at our Family Camp without the pressure to make them perfect.

Couples are often given solutions such as the following to manage busyness and disconnection:

Slow down. Do less. Create margin. Simplify your life.
Re-evaluate what is on your plate. Set better boundaries, shed
    commitments, and give yourself permission to say no.
    Delegate and be willing to let go.
Better manage your time. Plan your week. Schedule your calendar
    and rearrange your priorities to create space for your spouse.
    Make your husband or wife your top priority after God.
Schedule a date night every week and put it on the calendar.
Unplug from technology.
Limit your children's activities.
Create a marriage or family mission statement.

It's not that these ideas are wrong or ineffective. We'll hit on some of these things later in the book. Instead, these solutions often create a yo-yo effect for couples. They can provide an initial connection but are unsuccessful in maintaining a long-term bond. Disconnection slowly creeps back in and the guilt returns in full force. People end up feeling failed and discouraged.

So, relax. Take a deep breath. We aren't going to suggest that you book a cabin by the lake or add anything else to your already overloaded sushi plate. We won't give you a long list of things that you "should do," "need to do," or "must do" for your marriage that may push you over the edge. Moving from roommates to soulmates in the midst of busyness will not work by making big sweeping time-management changes or adding weekly date nights, holiday traditions, and couple's vacations.

Instead we want to follow the advice Moses gives parents on teaching God's commandments to their children in Deuteronomy 11:19: "You shall teach them to your children, talking of them when you are sitting in your house, and when you are walking by the way, and when you lie down, and when you rise." Notice he doesn't suggest "big" ideas such as formal devotions, Sunday school classes, four-point sermons, vacation Bible school, or mid-week club meetings. Instead, Moses encourages us to use ordinary moments to pass on a vibrant faith in God. We want to use the same logic for your relationship. We want to help you take advantage of simple bids for connection that can strengthen your marriage.

Micro-Moments of Connection

World-renowned marriage expert Dr. John Gottman has carefully studied thousands of couples for more than forty years. His research in the "love lab" at the University of Washington is some of the very best on the planet. In one study, Dr. Gottman discovered something astonishing while studying newlyweds during their first six years of marriage that we believe is a great first response to busyness. The couples who stayed married did *one* thing better than those who divorced: *They turned toward each other instead of away.* At the six-year follow-up, couples who were still married turned toward each other 86 percent of the time. Couples who had divorced averaged only 33 percent of the time.[2]

"What?" you might be thinking. "Turn toward what, who, or how?"

Gottman's research with the young couples uncovered something he calls "bids for connection." A bid is any positive action that you do to get your spouse's attention, affirmation, affection, or support. A bid indicates a desire for connection.[3] Gottman-trained therapist Zach Brittle explains the importance of these connection bids:

> Love is cultivated during the grind of everyday life. It's the
> seemingly meaningless little moments of connection that are
> the most meaningful of all. There is profound drama in the
> micro-moments of love. The time when Jack and Susan have
> dinner together and talk about their days rather than watch TV
> in silence. Or how Kevin and Kris tenderly touch each other as
> they pass in the kitchen. In these moments, we have a choice
> to turn toward our partner or away from them. If we turn
> toward our partner, we build trust, emotional connection, and
> a passionate sex life.[4]

To understand the connection bids that Dr. Gottman outlined, think about how children try to get our attention. Kids are much better than adults at being clear when they want to connect. "Will you play with me?" is an obvious bid for time. Jumping into your lap is a clear bid for attention. Even poor behavior like a tantrum can be a bid—*notice me!*

Throughout the day, we make hundreds of bids to create connection with our spouse. But unlike children, many of our bids aren't so obvious or well-defined. Say, for example, that your husband is a car fanatic and notices a Lamborghini Centenario driving down the road. He might excitedly shout, "Look . . . it's a Lamborghini! That's a 1.9 million dollar sports car!" Your husband isn't just drooling over an automobile; he's bidding for a connection with you. He wants some small sign that you are interested in what moves him. In a subtle way, your husband is hoping you will connect, however momentarily, over the car.

When Erin brings home new clothing that she bought off the clearance rack at Stein Mart, I (Greg) find it hilarious when she makes me guess the sale price for each item. I feel like a contestant on *The Price Is Right*! She holds up a blouse and excitedly begs, "Guess what I paid? It was regularly seventy-five dollars." I often roll my eyes hoping that Drew Carey will magically appear to give me some help. Over the years I've learned by trial and error to start my guesstimating at ten dollars. Erin seems to find great satisfaction in buying expensive items for less than ten dollars.

"I really don't know. I guess eight seventy-five?"

"Not even close," she excitedly counters. "It was originally seventy-five dollars, but I paid only six ninety-nine!"

Not even close? I think to myself, *I was only off by a whopping $1.76!*

The truth is that I've always had a hard time matching Erin's level of enthusiasm about clothing prices. I don't care about shopping. I hate going to the mall. It's just not my thing. I shop once a year at Dillard's year-end sale. However, I now hear Erin's sale price question as a bid for connection and not just a "price is right" game. Erin isn't trying to test my clearance rack competency; she's attempting to connect!

But bids are tricky, and it's easy to miss these seemingly meaningless little attempts at connection. Bids often appear trivial, like "look at the Lamborghini," or "guess how much I paid," or sending a quick text or link to a funny video or to something that you find interesting. Bids can be simple and underwhelming, like "Can you take the trash out," "You won't believe the day I've had today," or "I talked to your mother this afternoon." Bids can also show up as nonverbal gestures like a sigh, smile, or wink, a delicate touch, gentle shove, squeeze of the hand, quick nudge of the elbow, simple nod of the head, or a mutual look of understanding about a friend's quirkiness. And bids can be more obvious like

"What do you think I should do?" "How did you sleep?" "How was your day?" or asking for help with a sick child or prayer for a difficult situation at work.

When your spouse makes a bid, she is looking for a positive response where you show interest in her—even for the briefest moment. The key is to recognize a bid for connection when it happens, understand the deeper meaning, and then respond appropriately. Here are several examples of a connection bid and the hidden request—the message between the lines.

THE VERBALIZED CONNECTION BID	THE HIDDEN REQUEST
"How does my new outfit look?"	Will you affirm me?
"Can you put the kids to bed?"	Will you help me?
"Sit next to me."	Can I get some affection?
"Want to play a game?"	Can we have some fun?
"I had a terrible interaction with a friend."	Will you comfort me?
"Let's watch TV."	Can we unwind?
"I sent you a web link."	Will you take an interest in what I like?
"How was work today?"	Can we have adult conversation?
"Guess who I ran into today?"	Will you give me attention?

When it comes to bids for connection, it's not the *depth* of conversation, whether you like or dislike *how* your spouse is trying to connect, whether you're *interested* in the subject matter, or the *level* of intimacy that is reached that matters most—it's *how* you respond. When your spouse makes a bid for connection, you can turn toward, turn away, or turn against him or her. For example, back to the Lamborghini Centenario. When your husband excitedly shouts, "Look . . . it's a Lamborghini!" you can respond to him in one of three ways:

Turning away: You ignore his comment and silently keep texting your friend.

Turning against: "Who cares . . . like we could ever afford a two-million-dollar sports car . . . what a stupid waste of money!"

Turning toward: "Cool . . . I bet that thing is fast."

Remember, all he wants is some small sign that you are interested in what interests him. Turning toward your husband can take a few seconds, but in that brief moment you've shared a connection.

Author Ellie Lisitsa explains the powerful messages you send your spouse when you respond to her bid for connection:

I'm interested in you—you matter to me.

I see you trying to connect.

I'm open to you.

I'm listening.

I want to understand you.

We're on the same team.

I'd like to help you (whether I can or not).

I'd like to be with you (whether I can or not).

I accept you (even if I don't accept all your behavior).[5]

Unfortunately many of the bids that happen in a marriage are ignored or go unanswered—a hand reaching out for you to hold or a question that doesn't pull you away from your phone. This sends the unintentional message that you don't really want to connect. Worse yet, if you consistently fail to turn toward your spouse when he makes a bid to connect, eventually he will stop making bids altogether. Over time, the relationship plunges into loneliness. That's why learning to recognize these bids and responding by turning toward your spouse can make such a big difference in your journey from feeling like married roommates. It's not a cure-all, but it's a great beginning to re-establish connection.

Let's revisit our busy couple Nathan and Angela from earlier in the chapter to see how connection bids can make a difference in their marriage. After returning home from soccer practice and dance class, Nathan and Angela have retreated into the den to catch up on some work and Bible study preparation. "Nathan," Angela asks, "what's the name of John the Baptist's mother?"

As trivial as her question may seem, this is a good example of a simple bid for connection. Reading between the lines of her question, Nathan has been presented with a relational opportunity to strengthen his marriage, and it will cost him maybe ten seconds. Even if Nathan has no idea or doesn't care about John the Baptist's mother but responds, "Hmm . . . let me think," and after a five-second pause says, "Sorry, babe, I've got nothing," he has turned toward Angela and they've shared a quick connection.

In case you're a person who craves closure, the answer is Elizabeth, the wife of Zachariah.

We know you're busy. We recognize that you can't always be expected to drop whatever is demanding your attention in that moment and respond to your husband's wink as he walks past while you're straining spaghetti noodles. But sometimes you can. There are times when you can tear yourself away for three seconds and say, "Love you, too." You would have shared a micro-moment of connection. Notice and respond to these moments as they happen.

Letting a bid pass isn't going to bring your marriage down like a house of cards. One missed bid isn't the end of the world. Respond to the next one. Or better yet, if you can't act on your husband's wink, get him back when you don't have a toddler hanging around your leg. Walk by him and smack him on the butt. He won't mind—we promise! This isn't about guilt for failing to reach the 86 percent mark or feeling caught between the spaghetti boiling over and your winking husband. It's creating a new outlook on these seemingly mundane behaviors—to see these trivial actions as ways to connect. After all, isn't that what you want—to go from disengaged roommates to connected soulmates?

Remember, love is cultivated during the micro-moments—the grind of everyday life. Learning how to take advantage of bids for connection by turning toward your spouse is worth the small amount of effort that is required to respond in a positive way. We're not trying to eliminate busyness from your life or make you feel bad for not connecting. But you may need to re-evaluate what's on your plate and determine how to create margin, how to set better boundaries, or how to better manage your time. Those are worthwhile pursuits. However, at this point in your journey from roommates to soulmates, we want to help you take advantage of and maximize your bids for connection—yours and your spouse's. Maximizing your bids isn't a miracle cure, but it can reverse the rising tide of busyness and help you connect more frequently.

As author Jenna Jonaitis puts it, "A kiss, touch, or phrase tenderly reminds us of the love we have for each other. It makes time stand still and lets you forget about everything else for a moment. Even though it may be simple, the loving gesture speaks volumes. The time spent in all of the little things you give each other is what's priceless."[6]

Roommates don't have time for each other;

soulmates use simple, everyday moments to stay connected.

CHAPTER 4

Life-Giving Communication

Death and life are in the power of the tongue.

PROVERBS 18:21

Roommates talk about trivial things or "administrate"

their marriage to death; soulmates regularly

pursue life-giving conversations.

WHILE ATTENDING A MARRIAGE seminar on communication, Josh and his wife, Brianna, listened to the speaker declare, "It's essential that husbands and wives know the things that are important to each other."

Then, addressing the men, he asked, "Can you describe your wife's favorite flower?"

Josh leaned over, touched Brianna's arm gently, and whispered, "Pillsbury All Purpose, isn't it?"

Funny, right? But the speaker was making a serious point. Spouses need to know what's important to each other, and this knowledge only comes from communication. However, many people in roommate marriages say, "We just don't talk anymore." Relationship expert Dr. Amy Bellows explains why the absence of communication hurts a marriage: "Communication is the mortar that holds a relationship together—if it breaks down, the relationship will crumble. When spouses no longer communicate, a marriage nurtures no one. It is no longer a marriage."[1]

Research from the *TODAY* show and SurveyMonkey's "What American Marriages Are Really Like in 2017" found that 70 percent of Americans think good communication is the most important factor in a happy marriage.[2]

We seem to get the importance of communication, but it still remains a common struggle within marriage. According to the more than 800,000 individuals who have completed the *Focus on Marriage* assessment, the third biggest challenge that couples face is no meaningful communication.

Communication is complex and we need to become experts in it for a strong marriage. Good communication is tricky or it wouldn't be a top reason why couples divorce. A big part of the difficulty is that a single word—*communication*—is used to describe numerous important conversations that couples should be having. In many ways it's like the word *run*. Many linguists consider this three-letter word to be the most complicated, multifaceted word in the English language. "That's absurd," you might be thinking. It's true. According to the *Oxford English Dictionary* editors, the word *run* has the most meanings in all of English, possessing more than 645 different usage cases for the verb form alone, and the analysis took one professional lexicographer nine months of research to complete.[3] Three little letters have so much meaning because context is everything. Think about it. You run out of milk and make a run to the store. On the way, you almost run over a squirrel as he runs for his little life. Still shaken, you run a stop sign and run into the back of the car in front of you. Now your car doesn't run properly, and your insurance company is going to run-up their prices. After a quick run-in with the law, you realize that you've run out of time to pick up your youngest from school. However, you quickly run into the store only to discover that they've run out of milk! To make matters worse, someone runs into your leg with their grocery cart and puts a nasty run down your favorite black leggings. Things have definitely run amok and now you have tears running down your face and you desperately search for a Kleenex to blow your runny nose. And now you just want to run away! Context is everything.

In relationships, the word *communication* has the same complexity as the word *run*. When people talk about communication in marriage, they mean many different types of conversations.

- You talk about problems.
- You communicate about your daily schedules.
- You discuss your to-do lists.
- You express frustrations.
- You talk through finances and budget matters.
- You chat about your day.
- You gossip about the latest rumors.
- You give your opinion.
- You express your emotions and feelings.
- You converse about your hopes and dreams.
- You discuss solutions and talk about how to fix problems.
- You lecture your children.
- You negotiate compromises.
- You profess truth.
- You make snarky comments.
- You verbally banter.
- You talk about sex (baby!).
- You give speeches.
- You reveal your fears.

Communication means so many different things. We have to stop telling couples that they just need to "communicate" better or talk more. It's not about quantity or quality; it's about understanding several important conversations, their benefit to your marriage, and how to maximize their effectiveness.

Four Significant Conversations
1. Small Talk

This type of communication is lighter—sharing basic facts about yourself or life in general. Think of it as chitchat or shooting the breeze with your spouse when you talk about trivial topics. For example, I (Erin) called Greg at work the other day laughing about something that happened to me. I was supposed to meet a new group of women for a Bible study. I found the right neighborhood and navigated to the address given to me. There were several cars parked outside a house so I made my way to the front door. The door was cracked open with a sign that read, "Come in."

As an extrovert, I was pleasantly surprised as I scanned the room and discovered a house full of women I didn't recognize. *Awesome*, I thought, *So many potential new best friends!*

I spent the next fifteen minutes introducing myself around the room. Suddenly the host announced that it was time to start playing the game.

Game? I wondered to myself.

And then I quickly realized that it wasn't my new Bible study group—it was a group of women playing cards! I had entered the wrong house by mistake!

Greg and I shared a good laugh at my goof and then we hung up the phone. That was it—a brief, small connection.

It would be easy to dismiss small talk as frivolous or shallow. Certainly if your communication is dominated by small talk then you'd become bored and there would be little depth to your relationship. However, these conversations are of great value to your marriage. Discussing basic information and details of your day establishes a simple connection without requiring deep emotional vulnerability. It isn't possible to exist in a constant state of deep emotional intimacy and vulnerability within your marriage—it would be too exhausting!

View small talk in a new light. These are bids for connection (remember from last chapter). You can either embrace the connection (turn toward) or you can ignore the attempt (turn away). Often when I'm at work and Erin calls me on the phone, I'll keep typing on my computer as she's talking. "Uh-huh," I voice having no clue what she's saying. Erin will even try to trick me as evidence that I'm not really listening.

"The house burned down today," she'll tease. "I fell asleep again smoking a cigarette."

"Uh-huh," I respond. "That's nice."

Wait. What?

"I knew you weren't listening!" she declares.

Certainly I can't always be expected to drop what I'm doing at work, but these small conversations are what keep us connected during the day. I can choose to embrace the quick phone call, or I can let it slip away.

The point of small talk is the exchange of general information that establishes a simple connection without deep emotional vulnerability.

2. Work Talk

This type of communication is about managing your day-to-day life as a couple or family. It's overwhelming to consider the sheer volume of tasks and decisions that must be made each day to keep your family functioning. This requires that you have regular "business meeting–like" conversations. They're unavoidable. And once you think your day is scheduled, it seems like the variables are always changing. Robert Burns' adage is so true: "The best-laid plans of mice and men often go awry."[4] No matter how carefully your day is planned, something inevitably is going to go wrong.

In fact, we're confident that your life goes awry often—shifting and changing like sand on a beach. That's why it's critical to engage in Work Talk and regularly discuss daily routines and schedules, to-do lists, activities, obligations, social gatherings, financial and budgeting decisions, and medical choices.

It's astonishing to see the unexpected issues that constantly appear as we attempt to manage our family. Balancing careers, raising kids, and managing a household all generate a massive to-do list even before adding in the inevitable hiccups. It's no wonder couples feel like business partners— that you have more of a work relationship than a marriage. However, roommates end up managing these things on their own, like independent business operators, or they fail to communicate about schedules and plans. The goal isn't to wave a magic wand and eliminate the workload or interruptions. Instead, the key is to talk about these responsibilities *together*—as a united team. Jesus said it best, "Every kingdom divided against itself is laid waste, and a divided household falls" (Luke 11:17).

If you've fallen into a pattern of managing your life by "dividing and conquering" as separate individuals, it's understandable that you feel like married business partners. Work Talk helps you to efficiently and effectively manage your life as a communicating team.

It's easy to feel overwhelmed at the prospect of having to talk through all of your daily responsibilities and errands. Relax! We're not advocating that you talk about every single to-do list item. Certainly it's unrealistic to expect that every decision that needs to be made will be discussed. Instead, decide together what types of decisions need to be hashed out first. You don't want to find yourself saying, "I forgot to tell you . . ." or "I thought you were going to . . ." or getting stuck in the cycle of functioning independently.

Obviously if all you talk about are schedules and to-do lists, your communication would turn boring very quickly. But this is an important type of conversation to have. The busier we get, the more necessary it is to communicate with each other. Otherwise, we're left in the dark about upcoming tasks, appointments, or events. This inevitably ushers in needless conflict and tension in our marriages and leaves us feeling like married roommates. Be flexible and adapt to the ever-changing circumstances in a way that feels good to both of you—as a team.

The goal of Work Talk is to constantly communicate while you administrate your marriage and family.

3. Problem Talk

A third type of communication focuses on dealing with challenges that *will* surface in your marriage. Problems range from

- Simple problem solving
- Working through arguments, disagreements, frustrations, hurts with your spouse
- Growth opportunities—*iron sharpening iron* conversations
- External difficulties

As I (Greg) was writing this section, Erin called me from somewhere in Oklahoma, lost. Her GPS somehow led her the wrong way home from visiting my sister's family in Dallas, Texas. Erin didn't need an emotional connection or a funny anecdote about my day; she needed a solution— and fast! So she turned to her teammate, and I quickly opened Google Maps and found her exact location. I was able to map out a shortcut that would get her home and save her some drive time.

This type of communication is different from Small Talk and Work Talk—there is a problem that requires an immediate solution or a conflict or crisis that needs to be managed.

You may be wondering, *But how do we do this in a productive way?*

Great question! We will spend an entire chapter (nine) on managing conflict in healthy ways.

A Word of Caution . . .

It's really hard to keep these first three conversations (Small Talk, Work Talk, and Problem Talk) from controlling your communication. This is true because you don't have to create these conversations—they happen naturally. Conversations about unimportant matters occur without much effort. In the words of the great 1980s philosopher, Ferris Bueller, "Life moves pretty fast. If you don't stop and look around once in a while, you could miss it." Life *is* fast and you are constantly bombarded with schedules, to-do lists, financial decisions, and tasks necessary to manage your busy family. You also don't need to conjure up problems. These challenges happen unannounced because we live in a fallen world, and it can be tricky trying to get two imperfect and completely different people to live in peace and harmony!

However, if these conversations monopolize your relationship, you will slowly kill your marriage. This is a powerful reality of King Solomon's words, "Death and life are in the power of the tongue" (Proverbs 18:21). If the majority of your communication centers on talking about trivial matters, administrative meetings, or dealing with problems, spouses become uninterested in talking to each other. You are dealing with each other on a serviceable level rather than an emotional level.

In one study, researchers found that older couples (married fifty years or more) spent around three minutes in conversation during an hour-long dinner.[5] It makes you wonder if the years spent in small talk, administrating their marriage, and conflict eventually took their toll on these mature relationships.

Although these first three conversations have value for your marriage, they cannot be the only topics you talk about. *Death and life are in the power of the tongue!* Your communication will bring either life to your marriage, or it will slowly kill the relationship. The solution is simple: Your marriage must also include *life-giving* communication—but this conversation requires initiative. Again, the other three conversations happen naturally, so you will have to purposely make life-giving communication happen in your relationship.

4. Life-Giving Talk

The key for a soulmate marriage is more communication, not less. But it's just not about "more" in the sense of quantity. You could talk for hours without going deep emotionally or sharing personal, intimate details of your inner life. Sadly, the average couple spends less than four minutes per day in meaningful conversation.[6] However, a study in *Psychological Science* claims that people are happier when they spend more time discussing meaningful topics than engaging in small talk.[7] As marriage therapist Marcia Berger puts it:

> The art of marriage is really the art of keeping up to date with your partner, of staying on track with your own and each other's life goals as they emerge, exist, and change. It is about supporting each other and staying connected emotionally, intellectually, physically, and spiritually.[8]

Your marriage needs Life-Giving Talk. These conversations are about knowing your spouse's inner world and allowing your spouse to know your inner world. Research shows that those who share their intimate, personal selves (feelings, fears, doubts, and perceptions) with their spouses tend to have happier marriages.[9] But these conversations don't happen by accident. Small Talk, Work Talk, and Problem Talk will monopolize your time unless you intentionally make space for Life-Giving Talk.

But how can you?

The 10-Minute Rule

We use the "10-minute rule," coined by Dr. Terri Orbuch, to create life-giving communication in our own marriage. Studying nearly 400 couples over the span of thirty years, Dr. Orbuch discovered that happy couples tend to spend about ten minutes each day talking about meaningful things.[10] Unlike the first three conversations, the focus here is on meaningful topics and your spouse's inner life—what makes each other tick, things such as

- Affirming who your spouse is
- Noticing what you appreciate and expressing gratitude

- Reminiscing about the good times in your marriage
- Talking about emotions
- Discovering each other's love language and preferences
- Unpacking hopes and dreams
- Discussing spiritual journeys
- Revealing stressors, worries, and fears
- Talking about friendships and social relationships

It's easy to see why these conversations can make a relationship mean-ingful. They show a commitment to understand your spouse's inner life—her emotions, hopes and fears, needs and dreams. You're showing your spouse that he is the most important person in your life and that you want to know everything there is to know. But these conversations have to be reciprocal. It's not just about knowing your spouse but being willing to let your spouse into these parts of your inner life as well. The real you. The best communication happens when you reveal your inner world ("this is the real me") and your spouse fully embraces the real you ("I accept you"). This level of vulnerability and acceptance will help you experience a profound intimacy together.

I (Greg) asked Erin what questions I could ask her on a regular basis that would be meaningful to her. She instantly responded, "I can think of four."

"Don't rush," I replied. "Take your time and think about it."

"How many questions do you want?" she teased. "If you make me think about it, I'll come up with ten more!"

"Good point," I said, waving her off. "I'll take the four right now."

Erin went on to explain that she would love it if I'd ask her:

- How are you doing emotionally?
- How are things going between you and the kids relationally?
- How are things going between you and your girlfriends?
- What is one thing that God has been teaching you lately?

These four little questions have become a gold mine for getting to know Erin's inner life. I'll ask her these when we're driving in the car together, sitting at a restaurant, during halftime at our kids' games, while we're lying in bed, squished side-by-side on an airplane, waiting at the doctor's office, during a coffee date, on our favorite hiking trail, at the dinner table, while we're getting ready in the morning, or whenever we can find ten minutes.

I (Erin) asked Greg the same question, "What could I ask you that would help me understand your inner life?" Ever the jokester, his list started with, "Ask me how things are going between my girlfriends and me!"

Actually, the more Greg thought about what he needed to let me into his inner life, the more he realized that the questions that I like for him to ask me really didn't do it for him. Often when I ask him, "How are you feeling?" his response is "fine" or "good." It's like he's taken a vow of silence.

We're different in what helps us get into our inner lives. So, instead of a bunch of "touchy-feely" questions (as Greg calls them), he likes when I ask him, "What was the high of your day, and what was the low of your day?" Like inching your way into a steaming hot tub, this question allows Greg to slowly submerge himself into an inner-life conversation. As Greg warms up talking about the best and worst parts of his day, I then have more success asking him "touchy-feely" questions. The reality is that I still get access to his heart and inner life—it's just a different pathway than mine. We did eventually land on these questions that I regularly ask:

- What was the "high" of your day?
- What was the "low" of your day?
- What is stressing you out most at work and at home?
- What is one thing that God has been teaching you lately?

The most difficult challenge to having life-giving conversations is carving out the time. The first three types of communication—Small Talk, Work Talk, and Problem Talk—all happen organically and without much initiation on your part. This is what separates Life-Giving Talk from the other three. For this vital conversation to happen, you will need to proactively find the time. And that's much easier said than done. We realize that finding one single ten-minute block of time can be tricky and might feel downright impossible. Depending on your season of life and your unique set of challenges, your ten-minute conversation may look very different from ours.

What is the best opportunity for you? It might be when you're getting ready in the morning, strolling your baby on a walk, eating at the dinner table, waiting at the doctor's office, during halftime at a game, while you're driving to church, lying in bed, sipping coffee, exercising, doing chores, grocery shopping, or driving home from work. If the last idea caught you by surprise, it's because ten-minute life-giving conversations don't always have to be face-to-face (although this is the ideal). Dr. Orbuch discovered that these work over the phone, by email, or in person.[11] This is a game-changer if you or your spouse travels for work, has a long commute, or if you are a military couple.

Another way we encourage couples to reveal their inner lives is to ask each other conversation starters. If you're like us, you probably get tired of asking the same old questions or you can't think of new questions to ask each other. The good news is that we have an online article loaded with dozens of great questions (www.FocusOnTheFamily.com /conversationstarters). Here are some of our favorites to aid you in your ten-minute conversations:

- What one skill or talent do you wish you had learned but haven't yet?
- What three things have you done in your life that you are most proud of?
- If you could live one year of your life all over again without changing a thing, what year would you choose? Why?
- What happened when you made the decision to accept Christ as your Savior and Lord? Where and when did it happen?

- If you could change your profession and do something different, what would you do?
- If you had to take a paid sabbatical and couldn't work for an entire year, what would you most like to do?
- Are there any daring activities that you'd like to try?
- What are the top five qualities that you hope our children will have?
- Describe your ideal way for us to spend an evening after the kids are in bed.
- What are some of the ways you like to be shown that someone loves you?
- In what ways do you like to be romanced?
- If someone wanted to finance the start-up of your business with no strings attached, what business would you start?
- If you inherited $200,000, what would you do with the money?
- What do you think is the secret behind couples who have been happily married for more than fifty years?

Make a commitment to spend at least ten minutes every day talking about your inner lives—the things that deepen your understanding of your spouse and that allow you to deeply know each other. In 1983, the band Journey released the song "Faithfully." In that song, there's a lyric we love: "I get the joy of rediscovering you."

Take joy in rediscovering your spouse over and over. One lifetime isn't long enough to truly know each other because you're always changing. That's the beauty of marriage!

Roommates talk about trivial things or "administrate" their marriage to death; soulmates regularly pursue life-giving conversations.

CHAPTER 5

Gentle Neglect

Love doesn't commit suicide. We have to kill it.

Though, it's true that it often simply dies of our neglect.

DIANE SOLLEE

Roommates gently neglect each other;

soulmates protect sacred moments.

AND THEY LIVED HAPPILY EVER AFTER . . .

Pam was living a fairy tale with Jim. Their romance began after Pam's friend set them up on a blind date. The relationship was everything that Pam had longed for. She and Jim had so much in common. They both were adventurous and loved the outdoors—long hikes in the mountains were one of their favorite activities. Jim was caring and attentive. They had great conversations and dreamed often of their future together. Pam loved that Jim was extroverted. It was a nice complement to her laid-back personality. Jim somehow pulled off a surprise engagement—proposing to Pam at the top of their favorite mountain hike. The wedding was a wonderful celebration with family and close friends. After the honeymoon they embarked on their greatest adventure together as husband and wife, and for a while, everyday life seemed normal.

They soon welcomed home the first of their three children. As life got busier, neither one noticed the slow fade. Their love never faltered for each other, but over time their relationship slid down the list of priorities. Most of their conversations revolved around schedules, to-do lists, household responsibilities, finances, and the kids' activities. Most mornings someone was running late for work and their goodbye consisted of a faux kiss blown from across the kitchen. A stale greeting became the norm when someone returned home from work, running errands, or chauffeuring the kids. Their conversations were constantly being interrupted by their children or a chirping cell phone. Family dinners became a distant memory, with soccer practice and gymnastics interfering. Homework and getting three active kids to bed often dominated their evenings. After a quick email check, they usually settled on opposite sides of the couch watching TV or perusing social media. Most nights they fell asleep after checking sports scores, the latest news headlines, and Facebook and Instagram on their smartphones.

Jim and Pam are distracted and disconnected from each other. They rationalize that they'll be able to give the marriage attention after the kids are older, when things slow down at work, and when the budget allows for a date night.

When they talk about their relationship, Pam complains that she feels neglected and that Jim is emotionally unavailable. "All he wants to do is watch TV," she says. Jim usually counters that he doesn't feel like a priority and is constantly taking a back seat to her job, the kids, her friends, and everything else in their life. "Whenever we're together Pam is more interested in her phone than me."

Couples end up as married roommates for a variety of reasons. We've talked about exhaustion leading to disconnection—you can't give what you don't have. We've discussed how busyness keeps you preoccupied so you often miss small bids for connection. Constantly administrating your jam-packed life stops you from having life-giving communication. Here, however, we want to focus on how neglecting each other and neglecting the marriage leads to feeling like roommates.

As we talk about neglect in this chapter, we are not talking about abandonment or neglect that stems from a hardened heart. We'll deal with rejection and abandonment in chapter eleven. At this point, we want to focus on "gentle" neglect—too little attention or careless disregard.

Gentle neglect primarily happens when couples stop prioritizing their spouse and marriage. The deprioritization often stems from two issues—overloaded schedules and careless choices about "sacred moments."

This type of neglect involves intentionality—one spouse intentionally picks something else over the other spouse. We're not suggesting that the choice is made with malice intent or done in spite. It most likely happens from carelessness or laziness. Pam and Jim are certainly busy, but it's not the hectic pace that's the problem. Instead, they've settled into a harmful pattern that's very enticing. When time is available, they're not seizing the opportunity. They're trading couple time or connection moments for what we call "sacred space invaders."

Sacred Space Invaders

Remember the popular 1980s video game *Space Invaders*? The goal was to defeat waves of marching aliens by firing a laser cannon moving horizontally across the bottom of the screen. As the game progressed, the aliens marched faster and the music sped up, creating enormous anxiety for the player. Eventually the aliens would overtake your base and defeat you.

In today's world, you have plenty of those descending aliens that march relentlessly toward your relationship, trying to distract you and destroy important moments that keep you connected as a couple. Instead of being locked within a coin-operated video game console, these aliens are all too real. They include distractions such as

- Smartphones
- Children
- Television, DVRs, YouTube, Netflix, and countless other streaming services

- Work interruptions
- Computers or tablets
- Needy extended family members, friends, neighbors, or coworkers
- Social media
- Video games

These things are constantly competing for our attention, and we can access them 24-7. They interrupt us. They distract us. They cheat us out of important relationship moments like the marching aliens from *Space Invaders* about to overtake our marriage.

We're not suggesting that you can simply jettison these invaders. You can't get rid of your children. We heard a funny quote years ago: "We have met the enemy of marriage, and they're little." Our children require heaps of time and attention and seem to have a well-developed knack for interrupting us when we finally find some alone time. It's probably not feasible to move into a cabin that's off-grid to get away from needy people! It's not wise to ignore your boss. We're not suggesting that you purge your relationship of all electronics and social media.

These invaders are part of our lives. They *are* going to disrupt our relationship moments. The key isn't to dispose of these invaders; it's to learn how to protect our sacred times when they interrupt.

We see two main issues that cause someone to feel neglected or that result in the marriage relationship being neglected.

The first is what we call "unintentional" interruptions. These disruptions are involuntary. You aren't pursuing them; they seek you out. A young child who keeps getting out of bed while you and your spouse are trying to have a life-giving conversation. You're watching your favorite Netflix show together when your boss texts that she needs something for an important meeting the next day. You're a medical professional who must respond to multiple phone calls from the hospital during a family meal. A needy friend stops by when you and your spouse are having a coffee date. A car breaks down in front of your house and the driver needs assistance while you're chatting on the front porch. Your adult child calls in crisis while you and your spouse are on a walk together. An ex-spouse needs to discuss a parenting issue while you're relaxing together. The point is that someone or something interrupts you while you are connecting. You aren't seeking out the disturbance, but your valuable connection has been severed.

The above examples are different from "deliberate" interruptions. These are when you initiate the disruption. It doesn't imply that you are purposely trying to ignore your spouse. But even if the neglect is unintended, you are still initiating something that is taking away from your time together. Technology is the usual suspect when it comes to deliberate interruptions. Culturally, we've even coined a term to describe the accused: *Technoference* is the "everyday intrusions or interruptions in couple interactions or time spent together that occur due to technology."[1] For instance, in the middle of a conversation, one spouse accepts a phone call or responds to a text. His attention shifts from his spouse to his device. This severs the relational connection. As one author put it:

> By allowing technology to interfere with or interrupt
> conversations, activities, and time with romantic partners—
> even when unintentional or for brief moments—individuals
> may be sending implicit messages about what they value most,
> leading to conflict and negative outcomes in personal life and
> relationships.[2]

Another technology-related phenomenon that disrupts couple time is *phubbing*—the fusion of the words "phone" and "snubbing." This is when you feel "snubbed" because your spouse is distracted by his or her phone instead of paying attention to you. Your spouse is not fully present in the moment. For example, you pull out your phone to check the football scores while on a date with your spouse, read a text while at the dinner table, or look at Facebook when you're watching a movie together. Your spouse will feel invisible and that he or she is competing against a phone for your attention—and losing! Intended or not, the message conveyed is "You're less important than my phone."

The problem with deliberate interruptions is twofold. First, your spouse feels neglected. The word *neglect* comes from the Latin verb *neglegere*, which means "disregarded."[3] Ultimately, a neglected spouse will question his or her worth in your eyes. Second, your marriage is cheated out of face-to-face connection. Take smartphones for example. When you're both on your phone, you can be in the same room together and feel worlds apart. Researchers claim that we check our phones approximately once every six minutes, or about 150 times each day.[4] And the cell phone is a jealous lover—demanding attention all day through automatic notifications, calls, texts, Facebook, Instagram, YouTube, news feeds, sports scores, video streaming, music, and endless apps. Our cell phones and other things rob us of the precious moments that we have to connect.

Please don't misunderstand us. We're not picking on technology. Not all screen time is harmful to your marriage. Cell phones, email, video chat, and social media can help couples stay connected throughout the day via romantic texts, playful posts, funny pictures, and video chats. I (Greg) had to walk out of a meeting at work once because Erin sent me the funniest text. She received a Facebook reminder that it was someone's birthday. It was a friend she knew from several moves ago, someone she had "friended" that she hadn't been in touch with for some time. But, being the friendly extrovert, Erin posted a happy birthday message, wishing her a great day with friends and family. Shortly after writing on the woman's wall, another friend sent Erin a frenzied text, explaining that the woman had passed away about six months before. Needless to say, Erin was mortified. Laughing uncontrollably, I had to leave the meeting that I was running, as I imagined my poor wife desperately trying to un-post her birthday wish!

Frequent texting and quick phone calls help couples stay current on the day's events. Research shows that regular communication with a spouse through calling and texting makes people happier and more secure in their relationships.[5] We use screen time to communicate when we're *apart*. This is the key difference. It's when we're *together* that technology can distract and rob us of our face-to-face time—our sacred moments.

The "obvious" is the slow fade that happens when we quietly neglect our spouse and choose technology or other invaders over connection. Roommates gently neglect each other; soulmates protect sacred moments. Moving from married roommates to connected soulmates requires that you protect these relationship moments against sacred space invaders. These moments are like your home base in the video game. Don't let the invaders beat you by destroying your home base.

Protecting Sacred Moments

According to Greek mythology, Sirens were dangerous female creatures who lured sailors toward their island with their beautiful singing. The sailors' ships would then crash on the rocky reefs near the Sirens' island.[6] The Siren calls of smartphones, kids, television, needy family and friends, computers and tablets, social media, and video games can be dangerous to the health of your marriage when they steal your sacred moments.

In the epic Greek poem *The Odyssey*, Homer describes an encounter between Odysseus and the Sirens. Instead of trying to kill the Sirens, Odysseus told the crew to plug their ears with wax and ordered them to bind him on the mast of the ship. He told the crew that no matter how much he begged, they should not untie him. When they passed near the Sirens' island, Odysseus started begging his shipmates to let him go, but none heard him. After they passed, Odysseus let them know that they were now in safe waters.[7] You may be wondering what a 2,800-year-old story has to do with helping you protect your modern-day sacred moments. The point is that Odysseus didn't attack the Sirens directly or try to eliminate them. Instead, he evaded the temptation by ignoring their alluring call. In the same way, you don't have to wage war against smartphones, television, or other invaders. This isn't about eradicating your home of TV and cell phones or taking a technology sabbatical. For most people, that's unrealistic advice. However, if you believe that God is calling you to purge your family of technology, then by all means pursue His prompting.

We're suggesting a less extreme solution. Instead of battling technology, evade its Siren call during key relationship moments. As I (Greg) write this section, I'm sitting at our favorite coffee shop, Mission Coffee, in Colorado Springs. A good friend from work and his wife are seated at a nearby table having a day-date. As I watch the couple connect (not in a creepy, stalker way), I notice that they've put away their cell phones and the only thing between them and life-giving communication are two cups of coffee and one huge breakfast burrito.

I (Erin) recently challenged a client to delete her social media apps off of her cell phone for a season. I just received a text from her, "I was scared but last week I did it. It's been awesome. I'm so much more present with my hubby and family."

This is what we're talking about. Nothing extreme was needed. Our friends didn't need to cancel their cell phone contracts and Erin's client didn't shut down social media altogether; they just needed to evade the temptation—the Siren call of the ringtones and push notifications.

We love how 1 Corinthians 10:13 addresses temptations: "No test or temptation that comes your way is beyond the course of what others have had to face. All you need to remember is that God will never let you down; he'll never let you be pushed past your limit; he'll always be there to help you come through it" (MSG).

Just like every other couple, your relationship will be tempted by these distractions. Call them Sirens or aliens; they are ever-present in our lives and are here to stay. They will call out for your attention. But like our friends at the coffee shop, we can choose to ignore them during "sacred" moments—times when we are able to relationally connect. And God will give us His strength and will show us a way out when we ask.

Let's talk about these sacred moments.

We have 1,440 minutes per day. During a typical day, most people spend these minutes sleeping, working, running errands, doing housework, caring for the kids, commuting, relaxing, relating, playing, eating, and doing many other things. Obviously, not all of these minutes are "sacred," nor do they need to be protected.

When talking about your marriage, what makes a moment *sacred* is its connection potential. Sitting together at a coffee shop without kids gives that moment high connection value. Thus, it's an opportunity that you can take advantage of to strengthen your relationship. As opposed to managing a whiny toddler or preparing dinner while getting your children to stop bickering and finish their homework. These moments have low relational connection probability. As a matter of fact, most of your 1,440 minutes each day contain very few sacred relational moments. But they do exist. And the sacred space invaders are itching to distract you and keep you from taking advantage of these ordinary minutes and turning them into moments to connect and strengthen your marriage. The word *sacred* in part means to secure something valuable against infringement—to actively safeguard or protect it from invasion.[8] This is the goal: *Recognize your sacred connection moments and protect them from the Sirens and aliens trying to destroy them.*

A sacred moment is a specific experience that facilitates connection between you and your spouse. Your marriage is unique and will contain different sacred moments that consistently show up in other marriages. But there are three sacred moments that are especially worth recognizing and protecting.

1. Pillow talk
2. Parting ways (goodbye)
3. Returning home (greeting)

Let's look at how to protect these sacred moments from the invaders.

Pillow Talk

Pillow talk typically refers to the intimate conversation between lovers right after having sex. As romantic as that sounds, we want to expand the idea of pillow talk to mean enjoyable, life-giving conversation between spouses in bed.

After a busy day, couples desperately need meaningful conversation. But for many, the habit of conversation falls by the wayside over time. After twenty-seven years of marriage, we believe that one of the best moments for meaningful communication is at the end of the day—when you're lying in bed together. This is when couples should be talking about the highs and lows of their day, discussing emotions, snuggling, kissing, having sex, and praying together. Sacred space invaders wreck this moment! We confess that this is a huge issue for us. Instead of using this precious time to reconnect, our cell phones often hijack this opportunity. Honestly, we've created a nasty pattern of checking our smartphones just before we go to sleep and right when we wake up. When this happens, we shift our attention from each other and send unintentional messages about what we value most. We often find ourselves lying next to each other in the same bed but feeling miles apart. Sadly, we're choosing to discard this sacred moment.

As a married couple, we need an "inner sanctuary"—a special place that is set apart from the rest of the house—and even the rest of the family. *Sanctuary* means a place of refuge or safety—where someone is protected or given shelter. Your master bedroom *can* make a perfect sanctuary. Treating your bedroom as a sanctuary means that you decide on some ground rules. Take a hard look at what is distracting you from connecting in bed at night. Is it watching TV in bed? Do you invite or allow a child to sleep in your room? Are you absorbed in your smartphone? Together find a solution for whatever is hijacking your pillow talk connection. Maybe you need to move the TV out of your bedroom. Outside of a unique circumstance such as a thunderstorm, nightmare, or sickness, your children should be sleeping in their own beds. Teach your children to respect your alone time. They also need to be committed to your having a strong marriage. Whenever our kids see us kiss and bemoan, "Gross!" we joke by saying, "Affection helps keep our marriage strong . . . this is in your best interest." Besides being playful with our kids, we are also trying to send the message that they need to support our marriage—everyone wins when our marriage is strong.

If your smartphone is the biggest distraction, like it is for us, consider leaving it in the bathroom to charge instead of next to your bed. It's easy to get engrossed in your phone when it's right next to you. I (Greg) finish getting ready for bed so much faster than Erin, and it takes only seconds for me to get completely lost in a news app or a game of solitaire. And then when Erin gets to her side of the bed and sees me on my phone, she quickly checks Facebook or responds to a text. Suddenly it's thirty minutes later and now we're both feeling sleepy. Sadly, we end up using up our energy and time messing around with our stupid cell phones instead of messing around with each other!

Pillow talk is all about connecting before you go to sleep. Now, we're not saying that you need to stay up all night talking and giggling like you're having a sleepover with your BFF. It can be a quick ten-minute conversation. But as we said before, it can also involve snuggling, kissing, and having sex. We encourage you to end pillow talk by praying together.

I (Erin) really noticed this when I visited some dear friends. Before they go to bed, they leave their cell phones to charge in the kitchen. They maintain this attitude of "I don't even know where my cell phone is" throughout the day. That's so refreshing and inspiring. Are we really missing out if we put the phones away?

Protecting your pillow talk and using it to connect creates a positive feeling that you and your spouse will hold all night long.

Parting Ways (Goodbye)

"Parting is such sweet sorrow." This famous line from *Romeo and Juliet* illustrates both how painful it is to say goodbye and how sweet it is to think about the impending reunion.

We're confident that you experience the same sweet sorrow when you and your spouse part, right? Like the young lovers Romeo and Juliet, maybe you were grief-stricken early in your marriage. But as the years have gone by, perhaps your departing goodbye consists of nothing more than a quick "See ya later, sweetie" called over your shoulder as you're running out the door.

We know that it's not that simple. Mornings can be stressful. For legitimate reasons, this might not be your sacred moment. But many couples waste the opportunity to send their spouse out into the world feeling loved and connected.

Whether it's in the morning, running an errand, leaving for a trip, or taking your kid to practice, saying "goodbye" is a sacred moment because it's an opportunity to acknowledge your spouse. When we rush out the door, it gives the appearance of indifference. This makes our spouse feel invisible and taken for granted, which leads to further resentment and disconnection.

We're not suggesting that you need to make some lavish gesture before parting ways. Your husband doesn't need a face smeared with red lipstick. Your wife doesn't need you to dip her to the ground with a passionate kiss. However, there are a few things you can do that will help you take advantage of this sacred moment. Compliment your spouse. We love how God praised His son on the eve of Jesus starting his public ministry: "And a voice came from heaven, 'You are my beloved Son; with you I am well pleased'" (Mark 1:11). Wouldn't it be great if every time we parted ways our spouse knew that we were well pleased? I (Greg) remember a mentor telling me that he always compliments his wife before she leaves for work because he doesn't want the first compliment she hears to come from another man. I've never forgotten that sage advice.

Parting is also an opportunity to speak words of encouragement. When you speak encouraging words, you are putting courage into your spouse. Life is difficult. It's easy to lose heart and get discouraged. Encouraging words give your spouse extra courage and determination to get the job done. Encouragement is lifting up your spouse and affirming him to the point that he says, "I can do this!" in the face of something that might otherwise seem too challenging. We love King Solomon's counsel: "The words of a wise person are gracious" (Ecclesiastes 10:12, MSG). Be gracious with your encouragement.

A final way to take advantage of the sacred moment around departing is to provide affection. I (Erin) have truly embraced this idea. I will not let Greg leave our home without a kiss. I don't care if I have to chase him out the door, he is getting kissed! In a battle over "love" and "like," Greg has long told me he'd rather know that I like him. He says he knows that I love him because I promised that on our wedding day. Greg says he doesn't question my love. But there are moments that he begins to wonder if I like him. For my husband, kissing him goodbye is proof that I like him. He says that it provides reassurance of my commitment and passion for him (except if I haven't brushed my teeth yet!).

However, our favorite reason why we should kiss our spouse goodbye in the morning is that men who kiss their wives in the morning live five years longer than those who don't. Seriously! A study conducted by a group of German physicians and psychologists found that men who were kissed by their wives every day missed less work because of illness, had fewer accidents on the way to work, earn 20 to 30 percent more monthly, and live about five years longer than those who aren't kissed daily. According to the researchers, the reason for this is that the kissers begin the day with a positive attitude and it is believed that those who don't experience it go out of the house with a lack of confidence.[9] Apparently, the Germans are really passionate about their kissing. There are thirty German words for different kinds of kisses. One word, *nachküssen*, is a kiss "making up for kisses that have been forgotten."[10] When you are affectionate with your spouse before you part ways, this is the feeling that he or she will carry all day long. So get busy kissing or *nachküssen*(ing)!

Returning Home (Greeting)

Three of the best words in the English language are "Daddy is home!" When our kids were younger, I (Greg) loved opening the door and being mobbed by my children when I returned home from work. No matter what they might have been doing, in that moment, nothing seemed more important than greeting me with excitement and ravenous affection. Our "grand-dog" (our daughter and son-in-law's dog), Sammy, a 60-pound Goldendoodle, does the exact same thing when we visit or when they bring him over to our house. Sammy goes crazy when we first appear. He whines excitedly, his tail wags out of control, and he runs figure eights in and out of our legs. I always hope that our family cat, Fiona, is watching. Unless indifference and boredom warm your heart, she could learn a few things by watching how Sammy greets us. Fiona frequently shoots us a dirty look when we come home, kind of like, "You again! This is my house!"

Newly-in-love couples show the same kind of enthusiasm as dogs and kids. We were returning home from teaching a marriage seminar when we encountered a young couple locked in a passionate embrace right outside the security area at the airport. It was moving—like watching a military family reunite after a long deployment. The woman literally jumped into his arms. They were kissing, crying, and hugging. I (Greg) ended up next to the happy couple while waiting for our luggage. Erin had left for a quick restroom break. The young couple was standing there still locked in a deep embrace. The guy made eye contact with me so I smiled and said, "Long trips are hard. I'm sure you're glad to finally be home."

"It's great to be back," he said while squeezing her even tighter, "Although I only left yesterday, it felt like I was gone forever."

She enthusiastically agreed, "It was the longest twenty-four hours of my life!"

Just then, Erin walked up and in her most frustrated voice said, "You're still here!"

I laughed out loud. I knew what Erin was really trying to say. "You're still waiting for the luggage . . . what's taking so long!"

But compared to the young lovers, Erin's greeting sounded callous: "You're still here! I thought we'd agreed that you'd be gone when I returned home!"

We laughed all the way to the parking lot once I explained that their dramatic reunion had stemmed from their being apart for twenty-four hours.

How do you greet your spouse when he or she arrives back home? Does it look like that young couple at the airport or does it sound like Erin's greeting?"

Returning from a business trip, one wife greeted her husband at the Denver airport dressed in her wedding dress and holding a huge sign that read "I'd do it all over again. I love you." Married for fourteen years, she wanted to make her husband feel really important and special. She wanted to communicate, "I'm here for the long haul."[11]

Obviously, it's unrealistic to put on your wedding dress or provide a standing ovation and rousing applause every time your spouse returns home. Most of the time you're in the middle of something. It's not that you're trying to act like our cat Fiona—indifferent or uncaring—you're just in stimulus overload. We get it. No judgment or guilt. But these tasks or distractions leave you less aware of what's happening around you, and your spouse starts to think that you lack interest and feels neglected. Roommates barely look up to say hello, much less walk over to embrace their spouse when they return home. Which is sad since most people would stop whatever they were doing to welcome a visitor into their home. Why don't we do the same for our soulmate?

The point is that we have a sacred moment that is there for the taking, but most of us miss or undervalue its potential. Greeting your spouse may sound simple, but this small gesture can have a big impact. People feel valued—you took the time to say hello and acknowledge your spouse. A warm greeting sets a peaceful and positive tone for the rest of your evening.

So take advantage of this sacred moment. Stop what you're doing to greet your spouse when you are reunited. If you're the one returning, embrace your spouse first before your pet, your kids, or the TV. The goal is to make your kids yell out "Gross!" That's the evidence that you've greeted each other well.

I (Erin) have a good friend who unexpectedly lost her husband. I'll never forget sitting with her after the accident, and through her tears, her pointing at their front door and saying, "I'd give anything to have him walk through that door so I could throw my arms around him and kiss him on the lips. I'd never let him go."

Instead of ignoring your spouse when she returns home, checking your phone as soon as you get in the car, or watching TV in bed, give that attention to your spouse. This will likely require the establishment of mutually agreed-upon limits during sacred moments so that you can give the first and best of your attention to each other—not your leftovers.

Roommates gently neglect each other;

soulmates protect sacred moments.

CHAPTER 6

Living Separate Lives

Every marriage will naturally move toward a state of isolation.
Unless you lovingly, energetically nurture and maintain intimacy
in your marriage, you will drift apart from your spouse.

DENNIS RAINEY

Roommates live separate lives; soulmates are

two connected individuals who are even better together.

AT FIRST GLANCE, Jeff and Lindsey seem like a normal couple. They are raising two teenagers and one chocolate Labrador Retriever. Their house is a "fixer-upper" that they hope to flip someday for a tidy profit. They exercise in the morning, see the kids off to school, go to work, eat meals, work on the house, watch their favorite TV shows, attend church, enjoy the outdoors, participate in hobbies, and socialize with friends.

They just do these things separately.

Married for fifteen years, Jeff and Lindsey have slowly grown independent from each other. Jeff is immersed in his career as a small business executive, taking the kids to practices, and working on the house; Lindsey is absorbed in working as a nurse, raising their two children, managing household responsibilities, and socializing with friends.

After a whirlwind romance and wedding, they quickly had their first child. They never really had an opportunity to learn how to be a connected couple. Now, the majority of their time and energy goes into their jobs and children. Their primary mission together is to raise happy, well-adjusted kids who follow the Lord. They are great parents but lousy lovers. They are content sharing a home and bills but not an interconnected relationship. The only time they are together is at a child's sporting event, church, or when they need to discuss finances, logistics, schedules, or to-do lists.

Their marriage feels cold and distant—like they are speeding down two parallel tracks instead of living life together. Both being fiercely independent, the priority isn't the marriage relationship. Jeff and Lindsey occasionally fantasize about finding someone else, but they stay married because loneliness isn't biblical grounds for divorce (Matthew 19:9), and they don't want to hurt their children. They both came from broken homes and can't stand the thought of their kids experiencing the pain of divorce.

They want to regain the close connection that was present in the early years of their courtship and marriage, but they feel like their relationship is like the continental divide (a ridge of high ground that runs through the Rocky Mountains, sending some streams of water toward the Pacific ocean and others toward the Atlantic). Jeff and Lindsey's marriage has divided into individual "streams" going in separate directions. They have lost their sense of togetherness and can't seem to find their way back to a connected marriage.

But Jeff and Lindsey are far from unique.

Many married couples coexist as they lead parallel lives. Studies show that as high as 40 percent of married spouses complain of feeling lonely sometimes or often.[1] In a study of older adults, more than 60 percent of people who reported being lonely were married and living with their spouse.[2]

Living Alone Together
Every couple must deal with the ebb and flow of connection and closeness. The demands of life require enormous amounts of time and

attention. During busy seasons, it's easy for your marriage to lose priority, and it can be extremely challenging to connect as a couple. It's easy to feel like you're two ships passing in the night. For many couples, this type of separateness is related to a particular situation and usually lasts for a specific amount of time or for a short season. The real problem is when the distance lingers for weeks, months, or even years, and one day you realize that you're living separate lives.

This is what happened to Jeff and Lindsey. Their disconnection became chronic. Jeff was traveling regularly for his job, and even when he was home, he was working on the house, hanging out at the kids' practices, or investing time in his hobbies. Lindsey felt like she was managing the household and raising their two kids alone. As they grew distant, Lindsay felt abandoned, so she threw herself into her children, her job as a nurse, and her female friendships. Eventually, they had little in common and felt like they were living alone together.

As it happened with Jeff and Lindsey, a couple can be living independently of one another without even realizing that they are living parallel lives. Here are some warning signs that your relationship is speeding down parallel tracks:

- You hardly see each other when at home. You rarely share meals together. You spend most of your time in separate rooms of the house.

- Household chores get done independently.

- You spend most weekends, evenings, or time off invested in your children, your friends, church, hobbies, or personal interests.

- Your spouse isn't the first person you call to talk about your day or to share good news. If you are upset, you're more likely to confide in someone else.

- You don't check with your spouse when making decisions or discuss individual plans or activities.

- You go to bed at separate times and get out of bed at different times. You no longer sleep in the same bed or in the same room.

- You have separate bank accounts—"his" money and "her" money.

- You don't seem to argue anymore—why bother?

- Most of your conversations focus on everyday responsibilities and logistics rather than emotional and "inner-life" issues.

- Besides the kids, you seem to have little in common. You have separate hobbies and interests.

- You exist in proximity to each other. You sit on opposite sides of the couch when you watch TV. When you're in bed, you sleep on your own sides and never touch.

- Sex is rare or nonexistent.

- You hang out with your own friends and have hardly any "couple" friends.

- You don't function like teammates.

- You stay together for the sake of the children.

The sum total of these behaviors amounts to an efficient but lonely marriage. Marriage, by God's own definition, is about oneness and deep intimacy: *two united into one* (Genesis 2:24). No one imagines feeling alone in marriage while picking out a wedding dress. We're quite sure that you didn't stand at the altar thinking, *I can't wait to get married so we can live separate lives!* Nevertheless, a marriage can be a very lonely place.

A lonely marriage might seem like an oxymoron. The fantasy is marriage should guarantee a lifelong "best friend" so you never have to feel alone again. But marriage doesn't insulate us from loneliness. Living with a spouse doesn't guarantee connection. As one author explains:

People tend to think of abandonment as something physical, like neglect. A loss of physical closeness due to death, divorce, or illness can be felt as an emotional abandonment as well. But emotional abandonment has nothing to do with proximity: It can happen when the other person is lying right beside us, when we can't connect or when our emotional needs aren't being met in our relationship.[3]

In many ways, this type of loneliness is much more painful because you are *married*. Although you're physically not "alone," you feel extraordinarily lonely from the alienation. As one author explains:

When isolation infects a marriage, a husband and a wife exclude each other. When you're excluded, you have a feeling of distance, a lack of closeness, and little real intimacy. You can share a bed, eat at the same dinner table, watch the same TV, share the same checking account, and parent the same children—and still be alone. You may have sex, but you don't have love. You may talk, but you don't communicate. You live together, but you don't share life.[4]

Living solo isn't what we were created for. Our Creator has placed in us an irresistible longing to know and be known intimately. Deep within our very being God has planted this yearning to belong, for someone to discover the real person inside and make that relational connection. He put inside us the desire to be wanted and cherished as valued individuals. And this is especially true of marriage. "The LORD God said, 'It is not good that the man should be alone; I will make him a helper fit for him.' . . .The man gave names to all livestock and to the birds of the heavens and to every beast of the field. But for Adam there was not found a helper fit for him" (Genesis 2:18, 20). As he chose names, Adam certainly would have noticed that even the animals were paired up. This would have intensified the hunger deep within his soul for his own pairing—for a mate.

As we lead parallel lives, the detachment consumes our experience and creates a painful loneliness. Despair and helplessness overtake us and the marriage becomes unfulfilling. People get tired of trying to reconnect parallel lives. They grow weary of asking for more time and attention. At some point, exhausted people start fantasizing about what it would be like with someone else. And just like that, the marriage is in crisis. Even if the individuals don't recognize this as a danger zone, loneliness is a feeling that most people won't tolerate for long. We encountered this truth in our own marriage.

"I feel alone."

I (Greg) will never forget when Erin painfully expressed these words to me. We had recently gone through a difficult work situation. I was working for my parents' marriage ministry in Branson, Missouri. Working with family is never easy, but ministering together seemed to be going fine and God was doing amazing things in the lives of couples. And then suddenly the ministry took a turn for the worse. I made some mistakes as a young leader, and my family relationships became very strained. Erin and I felt that the best decision was to resign and strike out on our own.

This decision ushered in a dark and painful season for me. I felt rejected by my family and I became depressed. Sadly, I didn't handle my emotions well. I was consumed with my own pain and I began to withdraw from Erin and the kids. I isolated myself in my man cave. Erin had every right to feel lonely. We both were hurting and it took an enormous toll on our marriage.

Like us, we're confident that you may be sick and tired of the same old dance: You confront your spouse about the lack of connection. He gets defensive but tries to initiate a date night or meaningful conversation. However, the change is short lived. You end up feeling more hopeless and alone. Eventually, you stop bringing it up and accept that this is as good as it will ever be. Apathy sets in and your heart slowly begins to harden. We ended up in this same dance. But by God's grace, we learned some important lessons.

The good news is that you can come back together. You absolutely can reconnect after years of living separate lives. The first step, however, is to understand that you are *not* being asked to abandon your independence.

Interdependence

People who live separate lives have grown used to their independence and self-reliance. We aren't suggesting that you have to pick between autonomy and connection. These are two ends of the relationship continuum. You're aiming for a balance between these two points. The big lie in marriage is that your spouse should be *everything*—your best friend, pastor, confidant, lover, counselor, co-parent, playmate, financial planner, chef, housekeeper, chauffeur, dream maker, and security blanket. This is a fairy tale. God created us as individuals, capable of being full, whole, and complete in Him alone. God makes it clear that He sent His Son, Jesus Christ, for each one of us—to bring us abundant life (John 10:10). Christ is our everything! A strong, connected marriage will be made up of two healthy individuals fully dependent upon Christ.

As you journey away from separate lives and toward connection, the bull's-eye is interdependence. Real change happens when the pain of staying stuck is greater than the fear of facing your issues. You have to deal with the underlying problems and start doing things that unite you as a couple. So let's look at several underlying problems that may be keeping you stuck.

What Is Your Monkey Trap?

To catch a monkey, hunters use a hollowed out coconut with a single opening just big enough for a monkey's small, flexible hand. The coconut is then tethered to the ground or to a tree and loaded with bait—a slice of fruit or some other delicacy that would tempt a monkey. The trap is set.

When a monkey reaches inside the coconut and grabs the bait, he unwittingly discovers that he can't pull his clenched fist back through the opening.

Sadly, the monkey refuses to let go of the bait, even to his detriment.[5]

Clearly it was not the coconut that was trapping the monkey. Instead, the true snare was in the monkey's unwillingness to let go of what he was holding on to.

In much the same way, we suffer a similar plight. So often in life we hold on to things that trap and imprison us. And like the monkey, when we refuse to let go, we face dire consequences.

When Erin finally confronted me about her loneliness, I (Greg) didn't handle it well. I got defensive and then withdrew even more because I felt like a failure. I had failed at our family business and now I was failing at being a husband and father!

The first step for me was dealing with my own monkey trap—the thing that I didn't want to let go of. I love the advice in Psalm 4:4, "Be angry, and do not sin; ponder in your own hearts on your beds, and be silent." Instead of continuing to be angry at my circumstances and isolated from my family, I needed to spend some time understanding what was driving my withdrawal and depression.

I went to see a Christian counselor. One really helpful insight he shared was that when men are under stress, they generally respond by becoming more withdrawn and acting more as an individual.[6] That was exactly how I reacted to my pain—I withdrew from my family and I isolated myself when I was home. We also explored the deeper feelings of rejection I had experienced. I was holding on tight to the perceived injustices that I had suffered at the hands of my family. I was also firmly grasping the feeling of rejection. Through the time with my counselor, I better understood that I felt discarded by my family. I was able to seek out God's truth about myself and about my family.

What is your monkey trap? Like Greg, you might have been wounded by someone and can't let go of the hurt and pain he or she caused. For others, living parallel lives has more to do with having grown up in a broken home where you never saw a connected marriage modeled. You might not have a vision of how interdependent couples behave. You might exist in a marriage that feels unsafe. Perhaps there is high conflict, sarcasm, abuse, disapproval, or other unhealthy patterns within your relationship. Many couples have never developed long-term plans for their marriage and have no shared dream that they're pursuing together. This lack of vision can cause relational drift.

Remember, there is a difference between a short-term season of disconnection and living separate lives long-term. Short-term reasons are specific (e.g., new baby, caring for an elderly parent, job change) while long-term reasons are more vague and generalized. What are you holding on to that is keeping you living parallel lives? Perhaps it's one of the following:

Self-reliance. Are you fiercely holding on to your independence? Growing up maybe you had to fend for yourself so it's hard to depend upon someone else. Your belief might be, "I have to do everything myself because I can't trust anyone." So, you've convinced yourself that you shouldn't depend on anyone.

Secrecy. Are you hiding past abuse, financial missteps, infidelity, a past mistake, or ongoing sin? Secrets require some degree of disconnect. To keep a secret concealed, you have to compartmentalize your heart and keep that part hidden from your spouse. Otherwise, the risk is that a close connection might expose your secret.

Emotional Walls. Do you avoid intimacy or have a difficult time connecting emotionally? Do you have high, thick walls to prevent getting hurt? Love is risky. Maybe you grew up with parents who were neglectful or abusive. Perhaps you had a really bad dating experience in the past. As a result, it's hard to open up and trust that your spouse will be there for you.

Addiction. Are you clenching firmly to an addiction? Behaviors such as workaholism, drugs, alcohol, eating disorders, pornography, or shopping can monopolize your time and requires distance from your spouse to maintain the addiction.

FOMO. Are you snared by the fear of missing out? If you are worried that you may miss something exciting, then you prioritize everything and everyone else above your marriage.

Denial. Do you refuse to confront a lingering problem in your marriage? Maybe you're afraid to "rock the boat." The fear is if you peel back the layers of hurt and pain, you won't survive— your marriage will end. So, it's easier to avoid your issues and live separate lives rather than facing whatever caused you to detach in the first place.

Whatever the cause, just remember that most people will not stay in a lonely marriage indefinitely. Don't remain anemic or passive. Take this seriously and get help to deal with the underlying issues—your monkey trap. A date night won't bring you back together.

Focus on the Family offers a one-time complimentary consultation from a member of our excellent team of Christian counselors. We also have an extensive referral list of Christian counselors in your area. Call 800-A-FAMILY or visit www.FocusontheFamily.com/Counseling. We also have an amazing intensive counseling program called Hope Restored for couples in crisis. It has an 80 percent success rate for couples who were on the brink of divorce (visit www.HopeRestored.com for more information).

Our journey took time and God used it to change our relationship—and us as individuals. God ultimately redeemed this painful situation and over time, I (Greg) restored the relationships with my family.

As Greg dealt with his depression and feelings of rejection, together we also worked on our marriage. So, start with your own monkey trap issues, and then add in behaviors that create "twogetherness" in your marriage.

Twogetherness

Remember Jeff and Lindsey from the beginning of the chapter? They have been leading separate lives for years and have lost their sense of togetherness. A recent interaction illustrates the loneliness they feel in their marriage.

Lindsey had a difficult shift at the hospital as a pediatric cardiac intensive care nurse. "I had a sixteen-month-old patient code today," she vented to Jeff. "As I administered medicine, this doctor started yelling at me to push the meds faster. Which, by the way, was impossible because her IV line was so small. I'm not an idiot. I was pushing the meds as fast as I could. She yelled at me in front of my coworkers."

"Did you push back?" Jeff asked. "You know those doctors will run over you if you don't stand up to them. You should have told her, 'I'm going as fast as I can! You are welcome to do it yourself if you think it can be done faster!' That would have shut her up."

"Are you serious, Jeff?" Lindsey angrily reacted. "You always try to fix things when all I really need is for you to listen."

"I was listening," Jeff defended. "I'm just saying that you need to stick up for yourself."

"Whatever!" Lindsey shouted as she headed for her bedroom feeling *alone* in her pain.

When a couple exists separately inside their marriage like Jeff and Lindsey, the emotional isolation is tough to endure. The good news is that two people can regain a connected marriage if they work at it together. This isn't a quick fix; it's a journey. Think of how two railway tracks in the distance appear to converge—they seem to come to a point. Miles ahead, the tracks look like they join together—and so can your marriage. But it will take time and effort to build attachment.

We can build attachment through emotional responsiveness. Dr. Sue Johnson, who founded Emotionally Focused Therapy, one of the most researched couples therapy models, says, "The most important thing I've learned in the last 35 years is that the secret to loving relationships and to keeping them strong and vibrant over the years, to falling in love again and again, is emotional responsiveness."[7]

That's a powerful statement by one of the best marriage experts on the planet. Emotional responsiveness answers the question, "Are you there for me?" In her fantastic book, *Hold Me Tight: Seven Conversations for a Lifetime of Love*, Johnson says that emotional responsiveness has three main components that can be summed up with the acronym A.R.E.: *Accessibility, Responsiveness,* and *Engagement.*[8]

Accessibility: Can I reach you?

Accessibility is first recognizing that your spouse is trying to reach you (a bid for connection). It means that you are available and open to your spouse. The moment Lindsey started sharing her story, she was reaching out to Jeff. To show our spouse that we're emotionally available we tune in to her feelings. When our spouse is upset or troubled, usually there is an obvious emotion like fear, frustration, worry, anger, or sadness. However, there are usually deeper emotions going on at the same time that are more difficult to notice, like feeling unloved, disrespected, worthless, controlled, unimportant, helpless, rejected, abandoned, failed, or humiliated. Accessibility means embracing both the obvious and the deeper feelings.

Instead of judging, rejecting, or minimizing your spouse's feelings, embracing an emotion means that you stay curious. You don't have to agree with the emotion or make a change because your spouse is feeling a particular way. You're trying to communicate, "Regardless of whether your feelings make sense to me, they matter." Instead of telling Lindsey how to resolve her problem with the doctor at work, Jeff had an opportunity to connect with her heart. How different might their interaction have gone if he'd said something like, "It's incredibly frustrating to be yelled at in front of your colleagues." This would have shown that he was emotionally available. Jeff then could have tuned in to the deeper emotion. "It sounds like you felt humiliated when the doctor questioned your competency."

Accessibility welcomes those feelings, "Tell me more about how that made you feel." The reality is that Lindsey is fully capable of dealing with this problem on her own. Part of the challenge in their marriage is that both Jeff and Lindsey are incredibly self-reliant. They tend to "buck up" and deal with these types of issues on their own. Emotional responsiveness connects hearts together and helps us to "bear one another's burdens" (Galatians 6:2).

The Greek word for *burden* means something that is "heavy" or is too much for one person to bear.[9] The apostle Paul is saying that we shouldn't allow a person to be crushed under the excessive weight of his or her burdens. Jeff was presented with an opportunity to help carry Lindsey's burden—the pain of being humiliated at work. To bear your spouse's burdens requires that you are accessible.

Responsiveness: Can I rely on you to respond to me emotionally?

Beyond recognizing that they are hurting, people want to know that you care about how they're feeling. To state the obvious: When your spouse reaches out, *respond*. If your spouse reaches out and you aren't available, say, "I'm busy right this moment, but you are important to me. Can we have this discussion tonight?" Then honor your word and initiate the conversation later. Don't ignore your spouse and fail to respond to his bid for connection. Otherwise, you will continue as disconnected roommates living separate lives.

Responsiveness is all about empathy. Sympathy is when you feel bad *for* someone. Jeff could see that Lindsey was upset when she came home from the hospital. We're sure that he felt bad for her; he's not heartless. But empathy is much deeper than sympathy. Empathy is when you feel bad *with* someone—you imagine what she is feeling and place yourself into her emotions. You see the world through her eyes. Jeff's mistake was responding to Lindsey with a solution and not listening to the underlying emotions. Instead of empathy, he tried to fix her problem. When you hurt *with* someone and deeply connect with his or her heart, it sends a clear message that he or she matters—it says the person is valuable to you.

Engagement: Do I know you will value me and stay close?

Engagement is some action that gives your spouse special attention that helps him feel valued and connected. Sue Johnson writes:

> The dictionary defines engaged as being absorbed, attracted, pulled, captivated, pledged, involved. Emotional engagement here means the very special kind of attention that we give only to a loved one. We gaze at them longer, touch them more. Partners often talk of this as being emotionally present.[10]

Engagement is the special kind of treatment that is reserved only for your spouse. Engagement stems from seeing your spouse as a priceless treasure. Engagement means doing things that create connection based on your spouse's unique and immense value. Look for activities that require mutual participation—that create unity, bonding, and attachment. As you deal with the underlying issues for your separateness, you can now target these types of activities that create togetherness:

- Check with your spouse when making decisions and discuss individual plans or activities together.

- Call your spouse first to talk about your day, to confide in when you're upset, or to share good news.

- Have a weekly date night so you can have some fun together. However, make a rule that you won't discuss "hot-button topics" while on your date.

- Find a common hobby or shared interest.

- Prioritize sex. Oxytocin, the hormone that is released after orgasm, increases your feelings of trust and connection.[11]

- Cuddle on the couch when you watch TV and snuggle when you're in bed.

- Hang out with couple friends.

- Fight self-reliance. Ask your spouse what he or she needs *and* tell your spouse what you need.

- Develop a shared dream that you can pursue together.

Remember, this is a journey and not a quick fix. It will take time and intentionality for you to reconnect. But eventually you can overcome the separateness and loneliness. Barbara Cage said it best: "Love is a partnership of two unique people who bring out the very best in each other, and who know that even though they are wonderful as individuals, they are even better together."

Roommates live separate lives; soulmates are

two connected individuals who are even better together.

CHAPTER 7

Rekindling Romance and Passion

One of the biggest passion killers in a marriage
is the onset of tedious predictability.

GARY JACKSON

Roommates are bored and their passion has been
replaced by predictable routine; soulmates closely
pursue each other in exciting ways.

IN HIS TIMELESS BOOK *My Utmost for His Highest*, Oswald Chambers
wrote, "Human nature, if it is healthy, demands excitement, and if it
does not obtain its thrilling excitement in the right way, it will take it
in the wrong. . . . God never makes bloodless stoics; He makes us passionate saints."

We love the idea of "passionate saints" made in the image of an impas-
sioned God who loves passionately. God has lavished you with love. His
everlasting love is unfailing and nothing can separate you from His rich
love. He takes great delight in you and even rejoices over you with singing.
It's impossible to grasp how wide and long and high and deep is the love
of our heavenly Father. Notice the excitement and passion in our heavenly
Father's love: *everlasting, rich,* and *lavish*! We want that same passionate
love in our marriage. After all, isn't that part of why we got married? At

a recent wedding, we smiled as the young couple exchanged their vows: "I promise to keep our lives exciting, adventurous, and full of passion."

It's easy to expect endless passion and romance in a marriage, especially if you read the dialogue between King Solomon and his wife: "Love is strong as death, jealousy is fierce as the grave. Its flashes are flashes of fire, the very flame of the LORD. Many waters cannot quench love, neither can floods drown it . . ." (Song of Solomon 8:6-7). However, every relationship has peaks and valleys—every marriage has seasons. And for most couples, something happens to their passion over time. But why does our passion seem to naturally fade?

Tedious Predictability

The old saying "familiarity breeds contempt" is the idea that over time in a relationship, happiness fades and is replaced by disdain. In other words, the better we know someone, the more likely we are to focus on imperfections. However, for most of us, familiarity probably doesn't usher in contempt; instead it often breeds *indifference*. Many people work hard to "win" their spouse and then over time they become comfortable. They don't feel like they need to make much of an effort. It's as if the conquest of love has been completed and now they are consumed by daily life.

In this comfortable state, it's easy to prioritize newer interests such as a career, children, and hobbies, and then the marriage feels stale as we deal with mundane aspects of our relationship in light of these other more exciting pursuits.

This is exactly what happened to Carla and Fred. They have been married for ten years and have two children. At first, they went out all the time, laughed constantly, displayed affection publicly, and loved each other intensely. And then they had children. Today their life is overscheduled with responsibilities and obligations. Logistics, schedules, to-do lists, chores, work, and kid activities—the ordinary aspects of their dull life together—dominate their conversations. Their sex life has disappeared, and they hardly ever spend time together without their children.

Carla is frustrated in the marriage: "I love Fred but the passion is gone." Fred assumes that their sexless, stale relationship is just going through the normal ebb and flow of marriage. "It's just a phase," he explains.

Believing that this is just a "phase" is the real danger. What Carla and Fred are experiencing happens to most couples. After the initial honeymoon phase in the early part of our marriage, we settle into "the normal." As one author explains, "Most studies of love and marriage show that the decline of romantic love over time is inevitable. The butterflies of early romance quickly flutter away and are replaced by familiar, predictable feelings of long-term attachment."[1]

Think back to the early years of your marriage. Remember the honeymoon phase? This was a blissful time when everything was still fresh and exciting. When your spouse was still perfect, arguments were rare, romance was in the air, passion ran rampant, sex was magical, and you saw each other through rose-tinted glasses. Sadly, researchers have discovered that the honeymoon phase wears off after thirty months.[2] In fact, one online poll even found that it lasts exactly two years, six months and twenty-five days into a marriage![3]

As Carla and Fred experienced, researchers found that an initially high level of marital satisfaction steadily decreased after that period of time for most couples.[4] Why is this idealistic time short-lived? We become habituated to each other. The initial excitement of getting to know someone, experiencing new adventures, trying new things together, growing closer, and deepening the intimacy eventually fades away as we settle into routine. As one author explains:

> In the beginning, couples tend to engage in lots of novel and exciting activities together—what researchers call self-expanding activities. They dress up for dates, they explore new parts of the city, they try each other's hobbies, and they have

engaging discussions with each other. As time goes on, though, it can be easy for long-term couples to fall into such a routine that they stop doing fun new things together, leading to boredom.[5]

The couple is still very much in love, but they become accustomed to each other and are more likely to take each other and the marriage for granted. Thus, the passionate spark is extinguished as the marriage becomes familiar and predictable—boring even. In the beginning we date, woo, and passionately pursue each other. Then, over time, the passion deteriorates into routine schedules creating roommates who merely share a home, kids, bills, and problems. No wonder people become bored in their marriage.

Here are some signs that your relationship has slipped into predictable routine . . .

- The romance has disappeared.
- Marriage is no longer exciting—the spark has fizzled.
- The marriage feels boring.
- Passion has slowly faded into silent routines.
- You have stopped flirting.
- You no longer kiss passionately.
- Nothing is spontaneous anymore.

In her excellent book *Finding Love Again: 6 Simple Steps to a New and Happy Relationship,* Dr. Terri Orbuch conducted a long-term study of couples who've been married at least twenty-five years. She asked the following questions: "During the past month, did you feel that your marriage was in a rut (or falling into one)?" "Did you feel you were doing the same thing all the time and rarely doing exciting things together as a couple?" More than 42 percent said they "often" felt that way.[6]

Passion will fade . . . it's a reality. But we don't have to prioritize other "newer" things and allow our marriage to become boring and routine.

So, what's the solution? Marriage becomes special because you make it so. We have discovered something that has helped us deal with the routine that is inevitable in marriage. It's something we call *close pursuit*.

Close Pursuit

Unity. Togetherness. One flesh. These are great words to describe oneness in marriage.

But there's one word that often gets overlooked that is a game-changer for experiencing passion in your marriage. This word is found in the King James Version of Genesis 2:24: "Therefore shall a man leave his father and his mother, and shall cleave unto his wife: and they shall be one flesh."

The word *cleave* can have a powerful impact on your marriage. And we're not talking about using a meat cleaver! The Greek word for cleave (*proskollaó*) means to join or unite—to glue one thing to another.[7] This is the typical meaning we think of—a close marital bond that can't be broken.

However, recently we noticed the Hebrew definition for cleave, and it blew us away.

The Hebrew word for cleave (*dabaq*) means "closely pursued." It's the idea of following someone closely or intensely pursuing someone.[8] Which is exactly what most of us did early on during the dating years.

Our love story, like yours, started with passion and excitement as we got to know each other, laughed at new jokes and stories, displayed affection, experienced new adventures, tried new things, and grew closer together. However, once we were married for a few years, many of the fun, romantic, and crazy things we did while dating all but disappeared. In some ways, my (Greg) attitude was, *I won Erin. Why continue the conquest?* Like you, daily life consumed us. But over the past few years, we've been applying the idea of "close pursuit" within our marriage, and we've noticed how it's impacted our passion toward each other.

After years of marriage, what does that pursuit look like? We think there are two key aspects to consider.

1. Observe Your Spouse

"I've got this," I confidently stated to Erin on our date a few years ago. "She'll have the pepperoni and mushroom pizza."

Our waiter nodded and asked, "Will that be regular, deep dish, or thin crust?"

And before Erin could get a word in, I responded, "Thin crust . . . and bring extra parmesan cheese."

I smiled at Erin, proud of my in-depth knowledge of my wife after nineteen years of marriage!

As our waiter turned to leave, Erin rolled her eyes at me and corrected my order: "Do you have a gluten-free pizza?"

What? Gluten-free?

"Just put her gluten on my side," I explained, thinking that this would simplify the order.

"Umm . . ." Erin muttered looking dismayed at my stupidity. "Gluten isn't a topping. The cook can't sprinkle it on your side. It's wheat . . . the entire pizza crust is made with gluten."

Oh . . .

It's been eight years since Erin developed gluten intolerance. And since that day at the pizza restaurant, I've learned a lot about gluten-free living.

Which just goes to show that you will never perfectly know your spouse because he or she is always *changing.*

When life is crazy and chaotic, it's comforting to think that I thoroughly know Erin. It causes me to feel safe and secure in our relationship. But predictability is unrealistic. Change is certain. After being married for twenty-seven years, the illusion is that we know everything there is to know about each other. In one study, researchers found that the longer a couple had been together, the more confidence they had in how well they knew each other. However, the results showed that relationship length was a poor predictor of accuracy. In the study people thought they could correctly guess their partners' responses about 80 percent of the time. Unfortunately, they only guessed right 30 percent of the time![9]

Familiarity is seductive. Familiar things make us feel comfortable—safe even. But this "illusion of familiarity" can create serious problems in a marriage other than just getting the wrong pizza order. Thinking that you know your spouse, maybe you have no idea that he feels like a failure at work or that she hates cooking dinner.

Instead of assuming that you know what's important to your spouse, carefully observe him or her. Observing your spouse is important because he or she is of infinite worth and value. The biggest question is how will you handle the changes that are inevitable? Will change draw you closer together or will it drive you further apart? The key is to stay current and updated in your spouse's inner life—his or her likes, dislikes, dreams, hopes, and fears. Curiosity keeps the passion alive because it revives the interest, intrigue, and fascination that were present in the beginning years of your relationship. Get to know your spouse in new ways by paying attention and being inquisitive.

We've previously encouraged you to have a daily ten-minute conversation. Another fantastic way to "observe" your spouse is to ask about his bucket list—things he wants to do before he dies. We love discovering these unique desires so that we can become dream-makers.

God has placed passions deep in your spouse's heart. Rediscover these heart desires and work to help make these things a reality.

Continue to observe your spouse and pay attention to the details. But "observation" only gets you halfway there. You also need to "woo" your spouse.

2. Woo Your Spouse

Once you observe your spouse . . . you need to woo him. Wooing is some type of action that causes your spouse to turn toward you. It needs to be something that grabs his attention—a wholehearted effort to win the affections and favor of your spouse. The origin of the word *woo* is the Scots word "wow."[10] We love the idea of wowing each other. Rediscovering the passion and romance in marriage requires the wow factor—a quality that makes someone feel excited or surprised when he or she first sees something.

In the book of Hosea, we get a glimpse of God operating in the role of a husband. Hosea 2:14–3:1 is a fascinating look at exactly how God pursues His bride. Interestingly, the very first thing that God does is "woo" her. "Therefore, behold, I will allure her . . ." (Hosea 2:14). *Allure* means to attract by doing something flattering or desirable.[11] It's all about being attractive.

Think of a lure used to catch fish. Part of what makes a fishing lure so attractive are the flashy, bright colors; the noise it creates; and the action or movement it makes. A fish is induced to bite by a shiny, noisy lure with sharp action. The lure literally creates an unusual disturbance in the fish's normal environment that provokes it into striking even when it may not be interested in food.

If only people were as easy to allure. But the principle of attraction is still the same. What behaviors will mimic the lure's flashy attraction? How can we induce our spouse to turn toward us when many things are competing for his or her attention?

The rest of Hosea 2:14 says, "Therefore, behold, I will allure her, and bring her into the wilderness, and speak tenderly to her." Tenderness is a great way to woo your spouse. We asked couples at our live marriage event about what would allure them. Here are just a few of the more popular responses:

- Serving me when I ask for help
- Sacrificing time, comfort, or money for me
- Sharing laughter and playfulness
- Listening instead of trying to explain, argue, or defend yourself
- Showing politeness

- Observing you taking good care of yourself
- Giving me grace when I don't deserve it
- Seeking forgiveness for your mistakes
- Telling me that you still think I'm beautiful
- Participating in my hobby
- Flirting with me and seducing me
- Having my back and defending me to others

In Proverbs 5:19-20, King Solomon gives some excellent advice for married couples: "A lovely deer, a graceful doe. Let her breasts fill you at all times with delight; be intoxicated always in her love. Why should you be intoxicated, my son, with a forbidden woman?" We love King Solomon's encouragement. The wisest man that ever lived is telling us to always be captivated by your spouse. But for that to happen we must be *captivating*. Wooing a spouse is about being attractive—doing something flattering or desirable that will cause him or her to turn toward you. It's about captivating your spouse and acting like you're trying to get a second date.

Reinventing Date Night

Another important part of wooing each other is novelty. Familiar routine breeds boredom. We need new and fresh experiences in our marriage to keep our marriages strong. It's so easy to get stuck in habits and routines as we spend time together. Sure, time together is important, but researchers are finding that many couples are doing date night all wrong. Just being together isn't enough—routine won't elevate your relationship.

In one study, researchers found that couples who engaged in "exciting" activities (skiing, dancing, hiking, attending concerts or the theatre, etc.) reported greater satisfaction in their marriage than those who simply spent time with each other cooking, visiting friends, or watching a movie. The point is that it's more than just spending time together. Instead of doing the regular date night routine of dinner and a movie, exciting activities alter your brain chemistry by activating the brain's reward system, the same brain circuits that were ignited when you first started dating.[12] So recreate the old sparks of early courtship by doing something new, exciting, or unusual together.

The passion and excitement of the early years doesn't have to be a distant memory. Closely pursue your spouse. Become an expert observer of his or her inner life and woo your spouse into turning toward you. We wanted to close this chapter with a thought from author Vance Fry:

> The pursuit of one's spouse—the regular, ongoing nourishment
> of the relationship—can take so many forms as you walk
> through life together. Notes, flowers, and chocolates are still
> nice, of course, but the journey offers countless other moments
> to cultivate the relationship. Every day presents opportunities
> to pursue your spouse, to bless her, and to make her life easier
> in some way. Every day offers small pockets of time when you
> can connect, learn, and say, 'I care about you' in word and
> action. Every day is an empty page—a little note waiting to be
> written.[13]

Roommates are bored and their passion has been
replaced by predictable routine; soulmates closely
pursue each other in exciting ways.

CHAPTER 8

Spiritual Disconnection

When I have learned to love God better than my earthly dearest,
I shall love my earthly dearest better than I do now.

C. S. LEWIS

Roommates build individual relationships with the Lord;

soulmates build upon their personal faith to

experience a vibrant spiritual intimacy together.

MONOGAMY. Penguins are monogamous. Wolves stay together until one partner dies. Bald eagles and Shingleback skink lizards reconnect with their mate each breeding season. Even Schistosoma mansoni worms, a parasitic flatworm, monogamously pair off "'til death do us part." Then there's the poster child for monogamy: the swan. We've all seen the adorable image of the male and female swan with their necks in a perfect heart shape—they flock together for life![1] However, you've probably never given much thought to fish and monogamy. But there is one fish that mates for life. The anglerfish. Doesn't sound familiar? It's the nightmarish creature with the big mouth full of gnarly teeth and the glowing lure bobbing from its head. It was the same fish that chased Marlin and Dory in *Finding Nemo* while they were searching for P. Sherman's diving mask in the ocean's abyss.

But once you know more about these mated-for-life fish, you might not be too impressed by their particular brand of romance.

Male anglerfish are attracted by the female's bioluminescent lure. Once a male finds Miss Right, he latches on to her by biting her belly. Then their bodies fuse. Anglerfish couples take "the two shall become one flesh" idea a whole lot further than Genesis does. The couple's skin and blood vessels join together, and their bodies become so welded together that the male fish no longer needs to worry about seeing, swimming, or eating. He's literally one flesh with her, a mere appendage, entirely dependent on her for all his needs. Eventually his eyes, fins, and some of his internal organs wither, and he's just a sperm-producing lump attached to her for life.[2]

Male anglerfish monogamy makes sense now, right? You'd mate for life if you were nothing more than an atrophied lump of flesh hanging from your spouse like an appendage!

The anglerfish marriage is an extreme image of what our culture sells: *codependency*. Whether it's an anglerfish or *Jerry Maguire* ("You complete me"), our culture loves the idea that our spouse is our everything.

Throughout the ages, couples have been practicing this kind of co dependency. In Greek mythology, humans were originally made with four arms, four legs, and two faces. Because of their pride and their power, Zeus ordered them cut in half. According to the myth, every human spends his or her life searching for his or her other half.[3] However, as romantic as it sounds to have the type of love that the Greeks wrote about, we don't believe this is what God meant by the two becoming one flesh.

You might be thinking, *At least the church preaches a different message.* Are you sure? Many Christian wedding ceremonies inadvertently send the same codependent message during the unity candle lighting.

Couples often use the unity candle in their wedding ceremony to symbolize the union of two hearts and lives into one. Typically, two candles are placed on either side of a larger candle. The smaller side candles represent the bride and groom as individuals. The couple will take the individual candles and together light the large unity candle. We love this traditional wedding ritual up to this point. What happens next is where things go south. After lighting the unity candle, the bride and groom proceed to blow out their individual candles, symbolizing the end of their separate lives—the two becoming one flesh. Greg always wants to jump up and yell, "Wrong!" or "Stop!" I (Erin) have to gently place my hand on his tense leg and give him a look that clearly communicates that we will both be thrown out if he doesn't relax. Instead, in the receiving line, Greg just hands the newlyweds his card and matter-of-factly states that he gives them a few months before they'll need to call him for marriage therapy.

We're joking! Although Greg fantasizes about interrupting the unity candle ceremony, we applaud right along with everyone else as the couple is pronounced husband and wife.

Why are we picking on such a time-honored wedding tradition? We believe that the last part is a total setup for marriage failure.

As romantic as it sounds to merge the two hearts into one (like the anglerfish) or searching the world over for our other half, we don't believe this is what God intends. In the unity candle ceremony, if the only light that remains is the marriage candle, then the individuals no longer exist. And then it's inadvertently implied that we are no longer individuals and the marriage relationship is the priority—that's codependency. As we've said elsewhere, this is a huge problem because God created us, first and foremost, as individuals, capable of being full, whole, and complete in Him alone. When we de-emphasize the individuals and prioritize the marriage, we unintentionally move the marriage from a precious gift from God to an idol. This happens when our marriage relationship becomes the primary focus over our own personal growth as individuals. The only "eternal" aspects of the marriage are the two individuals. Jesus made it clear that there is no marriage in heaven: "For in the resurrection they neither marry nor are given in marriage, but are like angels in heaven" (Matthew 22:30).

Jesus came to this earth and died for *people*, not marriages. God is passionate about marriage, but He's more passionate about *you*. This is why we'd prefer that the unity candle ceremony keep the individual candles lit after lighting the center candle. The *individuals* (the husband and the wife) need to matter as much as the marriage. This is also why we started the journey toward reconnection in chapter 2 by focusing on individuals. Two full, whole, and healthy individuals are able to build a connected marriage.

We started with this truth because spiritual intimacy in marriage is built upon a vibrant *individual* relationship with Christ. It's in that relationship—that intimate connection with God—that we find purpose and completeness. Everything starts with God. That's how He designed it. God created us to depend completely upon Him—heart, soul, mind, and strength. God is our source—He is our everything. He fills us up in ways that nothing else can.

Spiritual intimacy in your marriage is built upon a dynamic individual relationship with Christ—our Savior and Redeemer. However, while many couples have their own individual spiritual relationships with the Lord, they don't have *shared* spiritual intimacy.

The Spiritually Disconnected Couple

Spiritual intimacy. These two powerful words have, at times, created pain and frustration in our marriage. Sure, as individuals we're always pursuing a personal relationship with Christ. But as a couple, there have been plenty of times that I (Greg) have felt guilty for our lack of a shared faith experience. As a Christian marriage expert, at times I've felt like a hypocrite. There have been seasons in our marriage when we didn't pray together regularly, attend church consistently, or have meaningful discussions about our faith. I would hear other couples talk about their close spiritual relationship and wonder what was wrong with us. Was I the problem? Was something wrong with our marriage? I always thought that this part of our marriage would be easy. When we first got married, I was in seminary. Accordingly, Erin assumed that we would share an amazing spiritual relationship together. Over time, Erin became extremely disillusioned with this part of our relationship.

Perhaps you can relate. Maybe busyness has consumed your marriage and you hardly have time to say "hello" let alone have devotions together. Perhaps your spouse resists when you want to pray together or battles with you about going to church. Maybe your spouse doesn't show any interest in talking about spiritual matters. Perhaps you feel like you and your spouse are at different levels of spiritual maturity. Maybe you are both passionate about your individual relationships with the Lord, but you do not share any real spiritual intimacy together.

Don't worry, you are far from alone. Spiritual intimacy in marriage can be a confusing and painful issue for many couples. As a matter of fact, in our own church-based small group, we recently asked couples to describe their shared spiritual relationship. Even though these were veteran Christian marriages, sadly, the couples either said that they weren't as close as they wanted or they weren't spiritually close at all. Why do we struggle to build a vibrant shared faith expression? As we look back on the spiritually "dry" seasons in our marriage and consider what we've learned from interviewing other couples, here are some of the main reasons why spiritual disconnection happens.

Spiritual attack. Never underestimate the battle that is being fought for your marriage—and realize that the main battlefield is your spiritual relationship. "For we do not wrestle against flesh and blood, but against the rulers, against the authorities, against the cosmic powers over this present darkness, against the spiritual forces of evil in the heavenly places" (Ephesians 6:12).

Differences. We all have different ways of connecting with God. Blending together two different ways of pursuing God can be challenging. In his excellent book *Sacred Pathways*, Gary Thomas has a quiz to help you both determine the unique way you like to connect with God. This information really helped us to appreciate each other's spiritual uniqueness and how to blend them together in our marriage. Visit www.focusonthefamily.com/marriage/growing-together-spiritually/differing-faith-expressions/your-spiritual-temperament-quiz to take this quiz. Using Gary Thomas' language, I'm (Greg) a "naturalist." I love learning about God by studying His Word and being surrounded by nature. To me, heaven is reading the Bible next to a cascading mountain stream! I'm (Erin) a "traditionalist." I connect with God through ritual and symbol (i.e., daily devotions, regular church attendance). I absolutely love the ritual of taking communion—it's like I'm literally communing with God in that moment.

Unsafe. Sometimes people feel inadequate and avoid talking about anything spiritual because they are worried about being embarrassed. Perhaps you or your spouse doesn't feel safe being open and honest about your faith. You may feel judged or criticized for your Christian beliefs or for how you practice your faith. You may relate to one or more of the following: You feel like your spouse is always "preaching" at you. Your spouse belittles your faith. You've tried to coerce, sweet-talk, or plead your spouse into a relationship with God. It's difficult to talk about spiritual topics with your spouse. Your spouse is constantly prodding you to do more spiritually.

Sin. Sinful behavior will impede your spiritual intimacy. To keep sin from being exposed, we hide and keep secrets. Thus, our heart is dulled toward God and we can't be deeply known by our spouse.

Spiritually mismatched. You are unequally yoked—one spouse isn't a believer or isn't religious. Maybe one spouse is going through a "dry spell" or is in a dark place spiritually. You are both Christian but practice a different faith tradition than your spouse (e.g., one is Baptist and the other is Catholic).

The impact when you don't share spiritual intimacy:

- Tension Sunday mornings as one spouse pleads for the other to attend church
- Resentment when your spouse forces his faith on you
- Hurt when your spouse prioritizes her Christian friends and activities over spending time with you
- Conflict over how to spiritually raise your children
- Lacking a spiritual vision or a higher purpose for your marriage
- Feel alone, unable to share the most important part of your life with your spouse

A shared spiritual relationship is a powerful force and can take us to the deepest intimacy possible. And science agrees. Researchers from Bowling Green State University found greater spiritual intimacy predicts better marital functioning. For both husbands and wives, greater spiritual intimacy was tied to greater warmth, humor, and love for one's spouse, less negativity and hostility toward the spouse, and greater satisfaction with the marriage.[4] They also found that couples with greater spiritual intimacy were more likely to work through conflicts in a positive manner and had a spiritual resource to motivate them to remain kind and resist the urge to "go negative" when they discuss their core conflicts.[5]

We really like how Drs. Les and Leslie Parrott describe the power of spiritual intimacy:

> For married couples, spiritual meaning should be a shared pursuit. Sharing life's ultimate meaning with another person is the spiritual call of spouses—of soul mates—and every couple must answer that call or risk a stunted, underdeveloped marriage. Like yeast in a loaf of bread, spirituality will ultimately determine whether your marriage rises successfully or falls disappointingly flat. The spiritual dimension of marriage is a practical source of food for marital growth and health. No single factor does more to cultivate oneness and a meaningful sense of purpose in marriage than a shared commitment for spiritual discovery. It is the ultimate hunger of our souls.[6]

So, how do we develop a deep, vibrant shared spiritual relationship in our marriage?

Shared Spiritual Intimacy

In life, we long to be deeply known. We want to be seen—thoroughly and completely. Intimacy is when we make known our innermost being. It's exactly what you get when you slowly say the word *intimacy*: into me see.

We believe spiritual intimacy involves a combination of two important parts: (1) pursuing God together as a couple and (2) mutually disclosing your own private spiritual journey with your spouse.

But this is much easier said than done.

Some of my (Greg) favorite childhood memories involve Saturday morning cartoons. I would stumble out of bed and head downstairs toward the family room TV to binge on Looney Tunes, Scooby-Doo,

Hong Kong Phooey, and Inspector Gadget. My path would always lead me by the living room—the "formal" space with all the nice furniture that I wasn't allowed to touch!

As I would pass by the living room (or the "museum" as my brother and I called it), frequently I'd find my dad on his knees in prayer or sitting in his favorite chair reading the Bible. My father had an amazing personal relationship with the Lord—one I've often envied. He regularly nurtured his friendship with Christ. My mom had a strong faith as well. However, I never witnessed how my parents cultivated a shared spiritual relationship together. I'm certain they shared a deep faith, but I really don't know how it worked or how they maintained it. I really didn't have a clue how this was supposed to work between a husband and wife.

As a couple, we certainly understand the importance of building a shared spiritual relationship, but this pursuit often feels like a rollercoaster ride—full of highs and lows, twists and turns, and it can be over in an instant. There are seasons in which we seem to be in a great spiritual rhythm together. There are times that we aren't connecting spiritually and Erin is disappointed in my spiritual leadership. There are moments that I'm frustrated at Erin or I'm hurt by something she did, and the last thing I desire is to connect spiritually.

Like many couples, we walked into our marriage without a clear sense of how a shared spiritual relationship was supposed to work. But over time, we have discovered three key experiences to help strengthen our spiritual intimacy as a couple.

1. Daily Disciplines

Second Peter 3:18 says, "Grow in the grace and knowledge of our Lord and Savior Jesus Christ." Daily disciplines are shared experiences that encourage spiritual growth between spouses. It's critical that we find ways to help us grow more like Christ *together*. It's challenging to have a shared spiritual relationship when we're at different levels of spiritual maturity. Thus, we need to find daily experiences that aid in our mutual growth and development.

One research study found that couples who shared the same faith and who regularly attended church services together reported a higher level of marital satisfaction. However, to us, the most fascinating finding was that when couples shared religious practices at home, which included reading the Bible together and praying together, the level of marital satisfaction was even higher.[7] That's amazing!

To reach those high levels of marriage satisfaction, we need regular experiences like . . .

Studying the Bible
Memorizing Scripture
Fasting
Listening to praise and worship music
Reading a devotional
Listening to a sermon podcast
Sharing about your own spiritual journey
Praying together

About prayer—praying together is so important to spiritual unity that we need to say a bit more about it. According to one study, regularly praying for your spouse has a profound effect on your own behavior toward your spouse. The researchers found that praying for your spouse leads to more cooperative and forgiving behavior toward your spouse.[8] As Brad Wilcox, the director of the National Marriage Project at the University of Virginia, explains:

Previous studies show that prayer helps couples deal with stress, enables them to focus on shared beliefs and hopes for the future, and allows them to deal constructively with challenges and problems in their relationship, and in their

lives. In fact, we find that shared prayer is the most powerful
religious predictor of relationship quality among . . . couples,
more powerful than denomination, religious attendance, or
shared religious friendships. In simple terms, . . . the couple
that prays together, flourishes together.[9]

You're probably looking at the list and thinking, *I don't have time to blow
my nose during the day. How in the world can we find the time to study the
Bible, memorize Scripture, or do a daily devotion?* The goal isn't to create
guilt that you "should" be doing more spiritual things together; instead,
these are daily opportunities that can really make a big difference in your
spiritual intimacy. Decide together which of these activities are realistic
for your situation.

These daily disciplines will keep you growing together in
Christlikeness. But if we had time for only one, we'd focus on praying
together and build this as a regular habit in our marriage.

2. Weekly Fellowship

Hebrews 10:24-25 says, "Let us consider how to stir up one another to
love and good works, not neglecting to meet together, as is the habit
of some, but encouraging one another, and all the more as you see
the Day drawing near." Weekly fellowship is all about time spent with
other believers worshiping God and growing in your faith. According
to a number of studies, married couples who attend church services
frequently are happier and are about 30 to 50 percent less likely to
divorce than those who don't attend church often or at all.[10] As Harvard
researcher Tyler J. VanderWeele explains:

> Our research . . . links religious service attendance to a
> number of better health outcomes, including longer life,
> lower incidence of depression, and less suicide. Our work

also indicates that religious service attendance is associated with greater marital stability—or more specifically, with a lower likelihood of divorce.[11]

VanderWeele further explains that religious institutions often provide various types of family support, including a place for families to get to know one another and build relationships, programs for children, marital and premarital counseling, and retreats and workshops focused on building a good marriage. Religious communities can provide important resources for a healthy marriage.[12]

Therefore, to keep our marriage strong and to deepen our spiritual intimacy, we need weekly experiences such as church worship service, group Bible study, prayer meetings, Sunday school classes, or small group participation. Over the course of our marriage, we have always been involved in a small group fellowship with four to six other couples.

Why does this help? Weekly fellowship injects Christian friendships into your marriage—people intentionally committed to building you up through encouragement, community worship, and spiritual growth.

Be intentional about developing close, intimate friendships with other Christians. Don't forget, "Two are better than one, because they have a good reward for their toil. For if they fall, one will lift up his fellow. But woe to him who is alone when he falls and has not another to lift him up! Again, if two lie together, they keep warm, but how can one keep warm alone? And though a man might prevail against one who is alone, two will withstand him—a threefold cord is not quickly broken" (Ecclesiastes 4:9-12).

3. Service Adventure

When the Bible talks about "one flesh" in marriage, it's about the covenant relationship that a husband and wife make with God. Once we make this lifelong commitment with God, we become "glued" or "joined" together in an inseparable relationship. One flesh is also about a synergistic relationship where you work together to achieve something far greater than was possible as individuals working on your own. It's the concept of the whole being greater than the sum of its parts.[13] A married couple should be able to leverage the strengths, gifts, and talents that both individuals bring into the marriage. That's synergy.

Matthew 28:19 says, "Go therefore and make disciples of *all* nations." This aspect of building spiritual intimacy is about exercising your "synergy" by spending time together in service of the Lord. We recently renewed our marriage vows with our four children and son-in-law in attendance. While at dinner together, our children were asking questions about our marriage. Our middle daughter, Murphy, asked, "What has been your best experience together as a couple?" I (Greg) lamented, "You want us to narrow down twenty-seven years of marriage into a single experience?" But without hesitation, Erin responded, "When dad and I get to minister together." My first thought was, "Why didn't I think of that!" But Erin was right on the mark. It's almost impossible to articulate the power of ministering together. For example, when we're up on the stage together teaching a marriage conference, I feel a profound sense of intimacy with Erin. Dale and Susan Mathis explain the power of serving together as a couple:

> There's a sweet intimacy that comes with working together
> on a service project or giving together to those in need.
> Couples who embrace God's call to serve others experience
> an added closeness, and there are special moments and
> memories that naturally come when you do things together.
> Moreover, participating together in ministry opportunities—
> whether in your church, neighborhood, community or the
> world—can also help you to grow in your faith as a couple.
> Working side-by-side to fulfill the Great Commission—in
> whatever capacity—deepens your spiritual intimacy like

little else can. Being the Lord's witnesses by serving, giving, encouraging, caring and loving as Jesus loved is rewarding beyond words.[14]

We need regular experiences such as . . .

Doing short-term mission trips abroad
Serving in the worship band at church
Working community service projects
Coordinating a marriage event at your church
Providing respite for foster care parents
Volunteering at a local ministry or community outreach

A service adventure helps you experience Christ in a new way and breathes life into your relationship with each other and intensifies your spiritual intimacy (i.e., guards against habituation, makes you more grateful, enlarges your perspective, puts your problems into perspective, gets you out of spiritual ruts, makes you step out of your comfort zone, encourages you to overcome fears, and allows God to stretch you). Find a cause that you and your spouse are both passionate about—something that benefits others and not just you—and give yourselves to it. We'll talk more about developing a shared dream in chapter twelve.

Dealing with "Dry Times" Spiritually as a Couple

I (Greg) experienced a very dark time spiritually in our marriage. A close friend, Dr. Gary Oliver's wife, Carrie, was diagnosed with pancreatic cancer. This couple was extremely important to us. Gary had been a groomsman in our wedding. He was my mentor and boss at John Brown University. They had been our mentors as a couple early in our marriage when we were struggling. Erin and Carrie had written a book together called *Grown-Up Girlfriends*.

Once Carrie was diagnosed, I found a ministry that donated "prayer pagers" for people going through a major illness. Instead of simply telling someone that you were praying for him or her, it allowed people to type in her number on the pager and it would alert her that someone was praying for her at that very moment. It was a wonderful source of encouragement to Carrie and Gary. Since we all worked together, we heard her pager go off constantly. It was so distracting (in a good way) because I would think how cool it was that someone was praying for her.

Carrie's prayer pager constantly buzzed for months. Although I knew that pancreatic cancer was a very difficult diagnosis with a bleak survival rate, I remember thinking that God had no choice but to heal her. I was familiar with the many verses about the power of prayer, and based on God's words, I was convinced that Carrie was going to be healed. How could she not be? Thousands of righteous Christ-followers were praying for her—night and day!

I'll never forget when I got a late-night call from Gary, telling me that his sweet Carrie was with her heavenly Father.

What? She died? That was impossible. I had witnessed months of unceasing prayer for Carrie's healing. How could she be gone?

When Carrie died, it rocked my spiritual world. I went into a real spiritual funk—especially about prayer. The verses seemed pretty straightforward. There's no ambiguity in them. "Ask and I will do it." How could God say, "Whatever you ask in prayer, believe that you have received it, and it will be yours" (Mark 11:24). It doesn't say "maybe" or "possibly." It says, "it will be yours."

I started to view prayer as more like a spiritual slot machine. Put your prayer quarter in the slot, pull the lever, say amen, and wait to see if this particular prayer would hit the jackpot. That's what it felt like to me. I would hear about people who were being healed from cancer. Why not Carrie?

I became a prayer cynic. Sure, God answered prayers, but the process didn't seem consistent with His Word. I was taught to pray like the persistent widow in Luke 18 who was asking a judge for justice. Even though the judge didn't fear God or respect men, the widow wore him down by being persistent. "Because this widow keeps bothering me, I will give her justice, so that she will not beat me down by her continual coming" (verse 4). The point Jesus was making in this parable was to pray persistently. That's what I witnessed with Carrie. But she still died.

Not only did this dark season impact my relationship with the Lord, it also impacted our marriage. Praying together as a couple had always been an important part of our relationship. My pessimism around prayer caused me to stop praying with Erin. It just felt shallow and fake. So, how do you respond when your spouse has a faith crisis?

Don't try to change your spouse. I so appreciated that Erin never rushed me. She didn't try to talk me out of my feelings or confusion. She listened to me and was patient. She let me question God without trying to provide the answers. I knew that it was painful when I didn't want to pray or go to church together. But she gave me the space to work through it. The Holy Spirit has to have room to move and transform hearts. Let Him do His job. Your job is to be a continuous conduit of love to your spouse.

Model a vibrant faith. First Corinthians 16:13-14 says, "Be watchful, stand firm in the faith, act like men, be strong. Let all that you do be done in love." First and foremost, it's your job to be growing more like Christ. Don't give away this responsibility to your spouse. Your faith is your responsibility.

"Let all that you do be done in love" means that your deepening faith allows God to love your spouse through you—through your open and well-cared-for heart. And God's love is always patient, kind, grateful, humble, polite, sacrificial, gentle, forgiving, protecting, trusting, hopeful, and committed (1 Corinthians 13:4-7). During my faith crisis, Erin continued to attend church and lead our family in prayer.

Pray for your spouse. We know this answer sounds cliché, but prayer is powerful. We love how Stormie Omartian explains the power of praying for your spouse:

> Something amazing happens to our hearts when we pray for another person. The hardness melts. We become able to get beyond the hurts, and forgive. We even end up loving the person we're praying for. It's miraculous! It happens because when we pray we enter into the presence of God and He fills us with His Spirit of love. . . . I've seen women with no feelings of love for their husbands find that as they prayed, over time, those feelings came. Sometimes they felt differently even after the first heartfelt prayer.[15]

Get community support. When your spouse is going through a faith crisis, it's critical to have support from your Christian brothers and sisters. "But exhort one another every day, as long as it is called 'today,' that none of you may be hardened by the deceitfulness of sin" (Hebrews 3:13).

Through Erin's support and prayers, I had an amazing encounter with God one day. I was working out by running stairs. I was frustrated with my relationship with God. I sat on the steps and started praying. I finally broke and accepted that I didn't have to know why Carrie died even though we had prayed unceasingly for her healing. I decided that it didn't matter. I trusted God and believed in prayer—even though I didn't always understand how it worked. Later that day, of all people, Gary Oliver randomly sent me a text quoting Romans 8:26-27: "Likewise the Spirit helps us in our weakness. For we do not know what to pray for as we ought, but the Spirit himself intercedes for us with groanings too deep for words. And he who searches hearts knows what is the mind of the Spirit, because the Spirit intercedes for the saints according to the will of God." These verses deeply spoke to my heart. I realized that I don't know what to pray for, but the Holy Spirit does and He knows God's will. And He is always interceding on my behalf.

Roommates build individual relationships with the Lord;

soulmates build upon their personal faith to

experience a vibrant spiritual intimacy together.

CHAPTER 9

Fight for Us

*It is sometimes essential for a husband and
a wife to quarrel—they get to know each other better.*
JOHANN WOLFGANG VON GOETHE

Roommates ignore problems and avoid issues;
soulmates use healthy conflict as an opportunity
for deeper understanding and connection.

OUR YOUNGEST DAUGHTER, Annie, loves to hear us tell stories of how
we fell in love. One of her favorites illustrates why I (Greg) fell madly
in love with Erin.

For several summers, we worked together as camp counselors in
Branson, Missouri. We weren't dating, but we would hang out as friends
during our off time.

One day, we were using our break time to swim around the lake
where the camp was located. It was late that afternoon when Erin
noticed a group of young male campers sitting on a dock with their legs
dangling in the water. Erin smiled because she knew exactly what they
were doing: *the Slew Lady.*

It was a tradition at the camp to tell the newbies the story of the
Slew Lady.

The story is about a mean camp cook who accidentally died in the lake when she went for a swim alone. But she was so despicable that she continues to haunt the camp by drowning campers who go swimming alone. Scary, right?

The point was to frighten the campers into not swimming alone. We're quite sure that many of the campers have needed therapy as a result of the story, but it was an effective method to keep them away from the water when they weren't supposed to be there.

Erin and I timed it perfectly. The sun was setting and the campers were deeply engrossed in the story. We hugged the shoreline and swam through some tall grass. We were able to quietly slip under the dock unnoticed. The prank was set!

We desperately tried to contain our laughter at the anticipation of scaring these boys. We swam directly under their dangling feet and waited for the perfect moment. Right when the counselor telling the story shouted the words, "Slew Lady!" Erin flew out of the water, screaming at the top of her lungs.

It was instant chaos. The young men let loose high-pitched screams that spooked wildlife miles away. The boys scattered away from the dock as fast as their legs would take them. They were truly terrified.

We couldn't stop laughing. I was so impressed with Erin's pranking skills! She became an immediate legend with the other male counselors, and I found myself even more infatuated with this deviously clever woman—or as I call her now . . . the Slew Lady!

Our daughter Annie loves to hear this story and how it ultimately led to marriage. Plus she's now terrified to swim alone!

We also enjoy hearing a good love story, and apparently we're not alone. Romance fiction generates over $1 billion per year,[1] and since 1978, romantic comedy movies have grossed more than $12 billion.[2] What is it about romance novels and movies that captivate so many people?

The formula for a successful romance movie or book includes something unexpected: *conflict*. What? Seriously. There needs to be a problem that creates conflict and tension between the main characters that threatens to keep them apart. We love to watch two interesting people in conflict to see how they will overcome their differences, fall in love, and live happily ever after. This is the classic Hallmark movie ending. Conflict is important in your love story as well.

Conflict Can Be Good

Troubles in marriage are inevitable—conflict is a natural part of any close relationship. It's not possible to take a man and a woman who God created so wonderfully different and expect that they will never disagree. You *will* argue, quarrel, wrangle, bicker, and clash from time to time.

Conflict can be a beautiful part of your love story, but most people avoid conflict and do everything within their power to avoid facing problems. Some people view conflict as a bad thing—that it's evidence of an unhealthy marriage. Others hate to face the challenges because they feel uncomfortable, they don't want to rock the boat, or conflict reminds them of past failures and disasters that threatened their well-being.

This avoidance ultimately sabotages the marriage. Problems are always "buried alive," and they often fester until they become much bigger issues. In the end, buried issues end up exploding like a massive volcano, leaving a marriage in its wake of destruction. Not managing conflict often causes long-term resentment, which eventually destroys unity and the feelings of love in a marriage. The apostle Paul recognized this difficulty among people when he wrote, "But if you bite and devour one another, watch out that you are not consumed by one another" (Galatians 5:15).

True peace comes from facing our conflicts and working through them in a way that feels good to both people. Marriage experts Scott Stanley and Howard Markman claim that successfully managing conflict is the key to staying in love and staying married. Their thirty years of research indicates that if couples learned to work out their conflicts, the overall divorce rate could be cut by more than 50 percent.[3] That's amazing! Who knew that actually facing our difficulties in a healthy way could produce such results?

Although successful romance novels and movies are built upon conflict between the main characters, few people in real life are genuinely excited about dealing with it. And yet, it's essential we recognize that these challenges create benefits in our marriage.

On the surface, our disagreements feel like a rocky wasteland—something that we should definitely avoid. But facing our problems helps us grow and evolve. Once on the other side, conflict has the potential to create greater understanding, trust, and connection. But many people don't view their conflict this way because these problems are unpleasant. Here are a few of the benefits we can discover when we face our conflicts:

- Greater insight into your own personal issues
- Better appreciation of the differences between you
- The chance to empathize with your spouse
- The opportunity to break old, ineffective patterns
- Restored unity and oneness
- Greater humility
- Learning to anticipate and resolve future problems
- Closeness as you listen, understand, and validate each other
- Deeper understanding, trust, connection, and respect—true intimacy
- Evidence of God's constant presence and help

Isn't this a great list of what conflicts can do if we face them together? The reality is that facing our problems doesn't guarantee intimacy; they only provide an opportunity for which deep connection can occur. Notice we used the word *opportunity*. As we deal with inevitable challenges, the key is to see the conflict as opportunity. When we talk through our problems, we get the chance to learn something about ourselves as individuals, our spouse, or our marriage. Instead of avoiding these conflicts, we can have the mind-set, "I'm thankful for this trial because we have an opportunity to deepen our understanding and intimacy."

You may be thinking, *Okay, I get it. Roommates avoid problems, while talking about them can actually deepen our connection. But how do we do this in a productive way?*

Let's explore why arguments happen in the first place and then how to resolve them in a way that feels good to both people.

The Anatomy of a Fight

Money. Household chores. Children. Sex. In-laws. We assume these are the usual suspects when discussing marital conflict. However, according to Dr. John Gottman, we're wrong. After studying 3,000 couples over a forty-year career, Dr. Gottman found that most couples fight about "nothing."[4]

What? When *we* fight it sure feels like we're fighting about something!

But it's not the big things that most often ensnare us; it's the little, seemingly insignificant things that create most of the conflict in our relationship—the little foxes!

Recently, we had one of these "nothing" fights. Our eleven-year-old daughter, Annie, had a soccer game. It was at a massive park that had around fifteen different soccer fields. And the place was packed with soccer players of all ages and their families. Needless to say, it was overflowing with people and cars. Greg couldn't find a parking spot. We weaved in and out of the different parking lots . . . nothing. Annie was getting nervous about being late, and she started telling Greg where to park. He loves it when our eleven-year-old daughter is back-seat driving!

The more Greg drove around, the more frustrated he became.

Greg finally found a place to park about a mile away from her soccer field. He had to parallel park in the last remaining spot on the street. As he maneuvered into the space, he kept hitting the curb. Cars were honking at us, Annie was moaning with frustration, and Greg couldn't seem to turn in properly. I (Erin) finally joked with a big wink, "Do I need to park it for you?"

I wasn't trying to be sarcastic or disrespectful. But at the time, my attempt at humor pushed my poor husband over the edge. In the middle of the road, Greg put the car into park, stepped out of the vehicle, and handed me the keys. "Fine," he barked. "You do it!"

I was shocked at Greg's reaction to what I thought was playful banter. Although Dr. Gottman says that we were fighting about "nothing," it sure felt like a big something!

It's the little arguments that multiply over the years that cause the most damage. Often, the petty fights are the result of miscommunication. But frequently we fight over trivial things when something else is going on at a deeper emotional level. Maybe we are exhausted from managing young children, frustrated at work, stressed out about an overloaded schedule, depressed about a difficult friendship, or holding resentment from feeling disconnected in your marriage. We often ignore these other hurts or frustrations, and they build to a boiling point. These things will eventually explode in some way—usually toward our spouse.

Pride Goeth Before a Fall

"Your mother warned me about this before we got married."

These are not the words you want to hear from your wife during an argument, especially after nearly twenty-seven years of marriage!

Apparently, as a young boy, I (Greg) was notorious for engaging my parents in long, arduous "debates." I wasn't trying to be disrespectful, but when something didn't make sense to me, when I didn't agree with them, or I felt that they were wrong, I would calmly engage my poor parents in lengthy "discussions." I learned from a young age that I could win one of these marathon exchanges by simply wearing them down. Eventually my parents would simply give in or give up out of sheer exhaustion. I was a little hellion in this way!

Unfortunately for Erin, I walked this style of relating straight into our marriage. I'm sure Erin and my parents bonded over this during the early years of our marriage—misery loves company!

I'd like to think that as I've aged and matured, these types of interactions have lessened; however, recently I found myself smack in the middle of one. But this time something changed.

Erin and I got into a discussion about our then 14-year-old son, Garrison, and his football-watching habits. I felt that she was being unfair to characterize him as *obsessed* or *addicted* for watching college football. Really, Erin was just trying to explain that she felt this area of his life was out of balance.

Well, needless to say, the accusation triggered a deeper emotional button in me, and we ended up in one of those grinding two-hour deliberations that I used to do with my parents. It's not that we yelled at each other or said hurtful things; I just exhausted Erin from the mental sparring and she eventually gave up. Sadly, I won out of attrition—I simply wore her down.

Erin started to climb the stairs toward our bedroom. She took a few steps, looked back at me, and said, "Your mother warned me about this before we got married."

And that was the end of our "discussion."

But her words really bothered me. Was this Erin's experience every time we argued? Had I really been doing this over the life of our marriage?

The next day, after a relatively sleepless night, we both apologized and worked out a plan around weekend football for our son. Although we resolved this disagreement, something still bothered me from our previous night's interaction.

At some point the night before, I'd suggested that these marathon debates were "just what we do." I encouraged Erin to accept this pattern, especially since we always work things out and eventually reconnect. In essence I was saying that the end justified the means.

Several days later, I was in a meeting with a good friend and colleague,

Ron Deal. We were talking about marital conflict when Ron made a simple comment that became an epiphany for me. Instantly I realized something about my arguments with Erin that completely changed my understanding of what happens. How I didn't see this before is insane—it has the mark of the enemy all over it!

Here was my epiphany. During conflict your heart closes into a tight ball—like a roly-poly. And a closed heart instantly begins to manufacture things that damage relationships: selfishness, arrogance, judgment, exaggerated or faulty assumptions, stubbornness, self-importance, rigidity, etc. However, the most destructive is *pride*. The first part of Proverbs 13:10 says, "Pride leads to arguments" (TLB). Conflict is rooted in a prideful, closed heart.

God hates a prideful and arrogant spirit. During conflict, a prideful heart is "self-consumed" and can't see beyond its own thoughts, opinions, perspective, pain, feelings, and needs. Again, picture that roly-poly, unable to see beyond its own protective shell.

In those moments of conflict, pride worries more about self—there is little room for a spouse (or even God). "In the pride of his face the wicked does not seek him; all his thoughts are, 'There is no God.'" (Psalm 10:4). As Ron and I talked, I realized that this is exactly what I do during these marathon arguments with Erin. I become so prideful that I'm unwilling to yield. However, I've never been willing to call it what it is: *pride!*

Over the years, I've blamed my parents, my personality, the way Erin harshly starts the conversation, or whatever, but I've never been willing to acknowledge my own pride and arrogance.

As I talked to Ron, I realized why pride is so relationally destructive during conflict.

James 4:6 says, "God opposes the proud . . ." God will oppose your pride—and so will your spouse! The word *oppose* means to compete against, face-off, do battle with—*combat*.[5] Aren't these perfect descriptions of what happens when we argue and fight?

Remember, conflict is good for a marriage; combat is destructive.

Healthy conflict can teach you something new about yourself, your spouse, and your marriage. This is the "opportunity" in conflict. Combat—things like sarcasm, yelling, escalating, criticizing, withdrawing, assuming the worst, stubbornness, debating—leads you toward frustration and relational disconnection. Pride always propagates combat and opposition.

Two specific ways pride can manifest during conflict are found in the first part of Philippians 2:3: "Do nothing from selfish ambition or conceit . . ." Selfish ambition is when you place self-interest ahead of what is good for your spouse. The Greek word for selfish ambition is *eritheia*, which means acting for one's own gain, regardless of the strife it causes.[6] Selfish ambition always produces rivalry that leads to feuding and division. "For where jealousy and selfish ambition exist, there will be disorder and every vile practice" (James 3:16).

Conceit is when you project the attitude that you are always right. The Greek word for conceit is *kenodoxia*, meaning that you are excessively proud of your own opinion.[7] This haughty attitude makes good communication difficult because there's no room for your spouse's perspective or for you to be wrong.

Both selfish ambition and conceit are self-focused and completely exclusive of your spouse. This is exactly what happens when I engage Erin in a marathon debate session. When my pride takes over, I'm focused on my interests and believe that I'm right. That's a nasty combination. No wonder these conversations feel so adversarial—like a college rivalry football game! Think Army vs. Navy, Michigan vs. Ohio State, or Oklahoma vs. Texas!

There is an obvious relational impact to marital combat, but pride also ushers in personal consequences as well: disgrace, humiliation, shame, discredit, punishment, dishonor, tarnished image, discouragement, fall from grace, and discord. Pride will keep your spouse in the role of adversary—in opposition against you. So, what's the alternative?

Antidote to Prideful Conflict

An antidote is something that corrects or improves the bad effects of something harmful.[8] Humility is the cure for unhealthy conflict because it's the opposite of pride. The Greek word for humility is *tapeinoó*, which means to make you less important—to be humble.[9] God gives His grace to the humble (James 4:6), and often, so will your spouse.

During conflict, we can swallow our pride and choose to value our spouse's thoughts, feelings, and needs above our own. This is true sacrifice—you give up your right to be heard first and focus on your spouse. This isn't easy or natural, but it will be a turning point in your disagreement.

Humility begins with self-awareness. Although simple miscommunication can ignite a disagreement, we encourage couples to assume that there is a deeper issue driving the argument and causing one spouse to react in self-protective pride rather than humility. Becoming aware of that deeper issue can help spouses find the humility they need to find common ground during conflict.

Back to our parallel parking fight. I (Greg) had been feeling overwhelmed at work and was feeling massively behind on a few projects. I didn't want to be at Annie's soccer game; I felt I needed to be home trying to get caught up on my overdue work. Erin's innocent comment was the final straw, and I overreacted. It wasn't about her playful remark; it was about me harboring stress to the point that I exploded. You bury alive every emotion. The hurts, frustrations, and stress that we sweep under the rug will work their way out somehow. And it's usually not pretty!

After exiting my car in the middle of the road, I quickly jumped back in and finished the parking job. I gave Erin and Annie a half-hearted apology, and we started the long walk toward the soccer fields in silence. At one point, Erin asked what was going on. At first I defended myself and blamed it on the crowded parking and Annie's back-seat driving.

But I finally humbled myself and admitted to feeling stressed out at work and feeling like I was failing at my job.

Revealing the real issue allowed Erin and me to have an honest conversation. Telling her about my work-related stress helped her to empathize with me instead of being mad at my temper-tantrum. As you humble yourself, often your spouse will extend you grace by honoring you—your thoughts, feelings, and needs. "One's pride will bring him low, but he who is lowly in spirit will obtain honor" (Proverbs 29:23). While pride ushers in opposition, humility creates support and favor—grace.

Talking about the real issue changes the conversation and helps you get to a deep level of intimacy. We know it sounds counterintuitive, but conflict can be the doorway into deep connection if you humble yourself and open your heart. Then from a humble, open posture the two of you can talk it through. But the focus has to be on the deeper issue that drove the minor conflict.

In addition to discovering the deeper issue for you, here are other ways that humility can manifest during conflict:

- I focus on you
- I give you my full attention
- I am patient
- I seek to understand you before being understood
- I listen with my eyes, ears, and open heart
- I assume the best about you
- I ask God to change me instead of trying to change you
- I recognize that how you feel matters regardless if it makes sense to me
- I treat you with gentleness and compassion
- I forgive you

Another powerful way that humility shows up in conflict is through x-ray vision.

X-Ray Vision

During conflict, pride also shows up as negative beliefs about your spouse. This type of negative selective perception is called *confirmation bias*. It's a way of subconsciously picking and choosing what you will and will not notice about your spouse.[10] When it kicks into gear, you start zeroing in on anything that tends to support your established convictions and beliefs while ignoring everything else. If your perspective is negative, then you focus on the negative. You notice what your spouse does that frustrates, hurts, or disappoints you. No matter what, you *will* find what you are looking for—good or bad. This is a form of pride.

In the TV series *Smallville*, Superman describes his x-ray vision as an ability to view a normally obstructed object with extreme clarity. What if we were to tell you that, like Superman, you, too, can develop an ability to see through obstructions? It's true. X-ray vision is a powerful gift that we can give our spouse. Pride sees our "rough exterior" or least-attractive tendencies: moodiness, anger, fear, laziness, a complaining or critical spirit, impatience, withdrawal, unreasonable demands, an obsession with control, etc. On the other hand, the superpower of x-ray vision allows you to see through the annoying qualities that your spouse is presenting and find the loving, joyful, kind, patient, faithful, good, gentle person your spouse truly is.

The true antidote for this type of pride (confirmation bias) is to see the positive—what is true about your spouse. And this requires humility. You have to *choose* to focus on the person within instead of dwelling on the rough exterior.

It's a powerful gift when you fight for your spouse's best self. X-ray vision in conflict is when you see your spouse as he or she has been throughout your marriage, not how he or she is showing up in the moment. While parallel parking at Annie's soccer game, I (Erin) had to choose to see Greg not as the angry person jumping out of our car to let me drive, but as the man he's been over twenty-seven years of marriage.

Greg has consistently been kind, honoring, and patient with me. That's the truth of who he really is. But it takes humility on my part to be willing to see this. For some, we know your spouse has made some horrible choices, and it may be difficult or almost impossible to see the truth of who he or she is. Make your prayer, "Lord, let me see my spouse through Your eyes. You see his/her heart, value, and true beauty . . . help me to catch a true vision of my husband/wife." The goal in this moment is to live out Philippians 4:8: "Finally, brothers, whatever is true, whatever is honorable, whatever is just, whatever is pure, whatever is lovely, whatever is commendable, if there is any excellence, if there is anything worthy of praise, think about these things."

In the same way, I (Greg) had to decide to see beyond Erin's "Do I need to park the car?" comment and remember who she's been throughout our marriage. The truth about Erin is she is playful, respectful, and loving.

Turning conflict from combat into something that will benefit your marriage flows from humility and grace. Our prayer is that you will see that your arguments are rooted in *pride*. And that God will give you the courage and strength to humble yourself.

Roommates ignore problems and avoid issues;

soulmates use healthy conflict as an opportunity

for deeper understanding and connection.

CHAPTER 10

The Sexless Marriage

Sex can be such a stark barometer for a marriage.

JOHN AND STACI ELDREDGE

Roommates rarely have sex;

soulmates have sex often in a way

that feels good to both people.

IN 1997, THE POPULAR NBC SITCOM *Seinfeld* released an episode called, "The Yada Yada." In the show, George Costanza laments about his girl-friend's use of the phrase "yada, yada, yada" to shorten her stories and leave out critical details. George ends up consulting Elaine, and they have this interaction:

George: *You don't think she'd yada yada sex?*
Elaine: *I've yada yada'd sex! Yeah. I met this lawyer, we went out*
   to dinner, I had the lobster bisque, we went back to my place,
   yada yada yada, I never heard from him again.
Jerry: *But you yada yada'd over the best part.*
Elaine: *No, I mentioned the bisque.*[1]

While we're not endorsing *Seinfeld* or glorifying premarital sex, it's fas-cinating how the show's use of the phrase "yada, yada, yada" helped turn the word *yada* into a cliché.

In today's culture, the phrase "*yada, yada, yada . . .*" is a disparaging response, indicating that something previously said was predictable, repetitive, or boring. It's the equivalent of sarcastically rolling your eyes and saying, "blah, blah, blah."

However, God intended to communicate something very different through the Hebrew word *yada*. In the Scriptures, *yada* means, "to know," as in sexual intercourse.[2] Sex is important to God. He never meant for *yada* to mean boring or predictable. After all, the Bible begins with a naked and unashamed married couple living in paradise with the instruction to "be fruitful and multiply."

God gave us this amazing gift so a husband and wife could experience the most profound and deepest level of intimacy and connection possible. One author perfectly describes how sex nurtures such an intimate connection:

> Sex brings a closeness that is beyond words. It relaxes you, puts you in tune with each other, and smoothes over all the everyday trials and tribulations. Sex is very much the glue in a marriage. You simply cannot get closer than having sex. It consolidates the bond that keeps people together.[3]

God designed our bodies to enjoy sex. We often hear Christians teach that sex is about serving the other person. But this one-sided view of sex misses God's full purpose. Sex is about *mutual* benefit. Otherwise, why would God furnish us with such pleasurable equipment? During sexual stimulation and orgasm, the penis is densely packed with nerve endings to tell a man's brain that what's happening is extremely enjoyable, and the woman's clitoris is the only human organ that exists for the sole purpose of pleasure.[4] These design features weren't accidental! Sex in marriage is meant to be fun. God even gave us an entire book in the Bible celebrating the sexual passion between a husband and wife. "Let him kiss me with the kisses of his mouth! For your love is better than wine" (Song of Solomon 1:2). Here the word *love* can be translated as "your lovemaking."[5] Your lovemaking is more delightful than wine!

God wants us to steward well this amazing gift. When there is consistent and satisfying sex in the marriage, the individuals feel close and connected. A Pew Research Center survey found that a happy sexual relationship was the second most important predictor of marital satisfaction, with 70 percent of adults saying it was "very important" for a successful marriage.[6] When there are problems in the bedroom, couples experience a profound level of dissatisfaction in the marriage.

According to the more than 800,000 individuals that have completed the *Focus on Marriage* assessment, sex is the top marriage struggle. The most common issue for couples is a mismatch in desire. This mismatch in desire usually sounds like this: "I have a higher sex drive and want more sex. I'm frustrated because she/he would be content if we only had sex once a month, which doesn't come close to satisfying me." As much as conflict around frequency is frustrating for both individuals, we think there is a bigger issue that is wreaking havoc all around the world: the *sexless* marriage.

The Sexless Marriage

A sexless marriage can look very different depending on the marriage. Notice how these four couples describe the pain and frustration of a sexless marriage.

> Doug has been dreading this moment. He noticed his wife's sexy pajamas and the perfume she sprayed on just before slipping into bed. Lying still, Doug pretends to be fast asleep. His wife places her hand on his chest and seductively whispers, "I know how to wake you." He lies still, faking sleep. He has no idea how to gracefully refuse his wife without her feeling rejected . . . again.

Beth enjoyed sex in the early years of her marriage. But working as a full-time marketing consultant, raising two young children, attending weekly Bible studies, cooking, and keeping the house clean have left her too busy and too exhausted for sex. As an early riser, Beth is usually asleep long before her husband. Their once active love life has become nonexistent. "I'm too tired" or "Maybe tomorrow" has become the normal response to her husband's advances. Beth feels guilty that she isn't interested in sex, but she feels overwhelmed at the prospect of offering that part of her when she is so depleted.

Forty-five-year-old Andrew feels emasculated. Although he runs a successful company, he can't perform in bed. Married twenty-three years, Andrew has never had a problem maintaining an erection . . . until now. As his wife flirts with him, he anxiously wonders if "it" will work this time. In his mind, erectile dysfunction happens to old men—not forty-five-year-olds. Embarrassed and unsure of how to respond as she initiates sex, he rolls over, pretending to be too tired. "In the morning," he apprehensively promises. His wife lays awake tearfully wondering why he's not physically interested in her.

As Jennifer's daughter turned nine, something happened unexpectedly. Up to this point, Jennifer would have described her sex life as normal. But now, the thought of making love to her husband is nauseating. Inexplicably, her daughter's ninth birthday has triggered Jennifer's own memories of sexual abuse at that same age. Jennifer is unwilling to talk about their sexual relationship, so her husband is left hurt and confused.

These stories, and many others just like them, expose a growing epidemic that is impacting countless couples across our country and around the world: *the low-sex or no-sex marriage.*

Although the definition isn't the same for every couple, the experts define a sexless marriage as having intercourse fewer than ten times a year, which impacts about 15 to 20 percent of couples.[7] And it's not just women who are refusing sex. One researcher studied sexually inactive marriages and found that it was the man who rejected sex in 60 percent of the cases.[8] Some people don't seem to care whether they have sex or not. Research suggests that around 20 to 30 percent of men and 30 to 50 percent of women say they have little or no sex drive.[9] Here are some typical signs of a sexless marriage . . .

- I can't remember the last time we had sex.
- Sex feels like a chore or duty.
- We hardly have time for sex.
- Sleep is more important than sex.
- We are great parents but lousy lovers.
- Sex happens only if it's scheduled on the calendar.
- Foreplay is a distant memory.
- We no longer kiss passionately.
- I keep getting rejected so I've stopped initiating sex.
- It's easier to masturbate than to have sex with my spouse.
- I don't feel close after making love.
- We never talk about sex or share our sexual desires.
- We've lost a sense of spontaneity and adventure in our lovemaking.
- I feel like the only one who shows any interest in having sex.
- Our lovemaking is boring—we aren't playful in the bedroom anymore.
- My spouse seems more interested in the TV or cell phone than in having sex with me.

- My spouse regularly looks at porn.
- I'm too resentful from working full time and then doing the majority of the housework and childcare to have sex.
- The Bible is used to pressure me into having sex.

What triggers sexual inactivity in a marriage? Let's start with kids. The presence of children can dramatically impact your sexual relationship. During the sleepless months after a child is born, many new parents are too tired for sex. A new mom will often have a difficult time feeling sexy after breastfeeding her baby. A new dad will often pull away sexually feeling slighted by his wife's reprioritized attention. With the obsession to provide our kids with every opportunity—sports, dance classes, community theatre, tutoring, music, foreign language lessons—who has time for sex? Plus, it's very difficult to have sex when you have a child peacefully snoring between you in bed.

There are a host of reasons other than kids for a sexless marriage. According to a study published in the journal *Archives of Sexual Behavior*, married Americans had sex sixteen fewer times per year in 2010-2014 compared to 2000-2004.[10] Why? The authors speculate that the drop in sex may be the result of stress and exhaustion from increased time spent working and parenting. Someone even coined the acronym DINS, which stands for "Dual Income, No Sex." Streaming entertainment like Netflix and YouTube is intensely competing for our attention and free time—and sex is often the big loser. We'll talk about specific reasons later in the chapter, but for now let's explore the impact of a sexless marriage.

The Impact of a Sexless Marriage

A sexless marriage impacts both the individuals and their relationship. The classic sex stereotype is that men have an insatiable sexual appetite and that women aren't quite as interested—that she is often "exhausted" or consistently develops a headache between 8 p.m. and 11 p.m. It's drilled into our psyche that men have sky-high libidos that create an intense urge to have sex *all the time*. And unless he's having a massive heart attack, a real man would never turn down sex. Certainly this may be true for many husbands, but it's not the reality for all men—especially as men get older. The truth is that women have the higher sex drive in about 20 percent of marriages.[11] A recent *USA TODAY* poll found that 20 to 30 percent of men say they have little or no sex drive.[12] But a man's sex drive is affected by many factors that have nothing to do with his wife. Issues such as lower testosterone, poor diet, stress, sleep problems, obesity, depression, medication side effects, lack of exercise, pornography, and drug or alcohol use will impact his interest in sex.[13]

However, this distortion about male sexuality makes his disinterest extremely baffling for a wife. If a "normal" man is highly motivated sexually, what does it mean when a husband isn't interested in sex? It's very confusing for a wife. When a husband rarely initiates sex or consistently rebuffs her advances, a wife may get suspicious: "Is he addicted to porn? Is he having an affair?" She may even wonder if his lack of interest means that he is secretly gay. It's easy to jump to these conclusions because then *he* is the problem. If it's not him, then it's *her*. The fear is "he's not attracted to *me*." When a husband isn't interested in sex, the most painful explanation is "I'm not pretty enough, fit enough, sexy enough, or desirable enough." In this male hyper-sexualized culture, it must be that she is defective in some way or not good enough. As one wife writes:

> Being denied sex by a spouse is one of the most painful
> and humiliating experiences one can endure. The physical
> withdrawal alone is torture, but worse is the emotional trauma
> of feeling that the person you have sworn to love all your life
> would turn his back on you. He might as well drive a stake
> through your heart with a note on it: "I don't love you. I don't
> want you. I don't need you."[14]

Being constantly rejected by your spouse creates massive insecurity in the heart of a woman. Sure women want to feel loved, but they also want to feel beautiful, pursued, and wanted by the one man who matters most. Every wife wants her husband to be captivated by her beauty—both inside and out. She wants her man to desire her sexually. And when this yearning is absent and her advances are rejected, she is left with a painful secret: *He doesn't want me anymore.* And this is a shameful and vulnerable place to exist.

A husband feels frustrated and discouraged when his wife repeatedly rejects his bid for sex. It creates deep resentment when he feels that she places the children, her career, girlfriends, and other pursuits above him and his desire to make love. A man will often personalize his wife's sexual rejection. Marriage researcher Shaunti Feldhahn, in her excellent book, *For Women Only: What You Need to Know About the Inner Lives of Men,* found that when a wife responds, "Not tonight," men really hear, "I'm not interested in *you.*"[15]A man wants to know that his wife is sexually interested in *him.* Deep within a man's heart is an inescapable longing to be wanted by his wife. Shaunti Feldhahn explains this deep desire:

> Sex gives them an increasing sense of confidence and well-being that carries over into every other area of his life. The opposite is also true. When a husband doesn't feel desired by his wife . . . he not only feels his wife is rejecting him physically, but that she is somehow rejecting his life as a husband, provider and man.[16]

It's the same sentiment that the all-male band Cheap Trick sang: "I want you to want me." Most men have a hard time admitting this desire or aren't aware that it exists, but it's exactly why they love it when their wife initiates sex and is an enthusiastic participant—the message is "I want you."

A sexless relationship impacts the wife and husband as individuals, but it also affects the marriage. Relationally, the bedroom becomes a war zone. The master bedroom should be a place of refuge from the stresses of life and the demands of our children (a sacred space). It should be a place where we stay current with our spouse's inner life. And it should be a playground for sexual intimacy. But a lack of sex often leads to a lack of emotional connection and closeness.

A lack of sex and the constant rejection often turn into blame, bitterness, and resentment. These deeply painful emotions eventually will turn into loneliness. Weeks and months turn into years. The longer a relationship goes without sex, the more difficult it is to revive the sex life. But it can be done!

Resurrecting Sex

A car that's in great shape physically and mechanically, but has been left to sit for a while, can develop all kinds of problems. After long periods of inactivity, the car may not start or run, it can develop rust, leak fluids, or spew noxious smoke. In the same way, the longer you go without sex, the more problems arise, and the harder it can be to reawaken this aspect of your intimacy.

Avoidance becomes a deeply entrenched coping behavior in the relationship that is hard to break and can cause other serious problems. When your car has been inactive, you take it to a mechanic. However, sexless couples aren't sure how to start the process or initiate the conversation. In the past, discussions about sex have quickly deteriorated into painful conflict and the fear is further rocking the proverbial boat. So these couples often linger in silence and choose sexlessness over dealing with the hurt feelings and underlying issues.

Just as you can get a car back on the road after periods of inactivity, your sexual relationship can be resurrected. There is always hope. We serve an amazing God who is passionate about sex. Status quo in the bedroom doesn't have to be your reality any longer. You can revitalize your sexual intimacy.

According to one online data expert, the top-searched marriage complaint on Google is "sexless marriage." And searches for "sexless marriage" are three and a half times more common than "unhappy marriage" and *eight* times more frequent than "loveless marriage."[17] Many of those searching for answers will discover a range of advice for fixing a sexless marriage—some good, some bad, and some downright ugly. Quick solutions like "just do it," schedule sex, sleep naked, plan an erotic date night, try new positions, take turns initiating sex, and talk about fantasies often don't work—at least not for long. Like rearranging deck chairs on the Titanic, these are temporary solutions to a deeper problem.

When we counsel a sexless couple, the first question they sheepishly ask is, "How often should we be having sex?" People seem fascinated by this question. A simple Google search reveals more than 40,700,000 results! The couples are really asking, "Compared to other couples, are we normal?" The "right number" of times to have sex is a tricky and loaded question.

I (Erin) remember being part of a Bible study group where the leader wanted to encourage the women to initiate sex with their husbands. Every woman was given a jar and encouraged to put a quarter in every time they had sex. The leader then instructed us to bring our over-stuffed jars back in two weeks. I self-consciously looked around the room. Some women high-fived their friends while others were unsure of how to respond, and a few looked extremely uncomfortable. It was the most awkward moment that I've ever had at a Bible study. Although I understood the purpose, this friendly competition seemed so insensitive because there are so many factors that impact how often couples have sex.

But if you are just dying to know the answer, here is what the research reveals. The average married American couple reports having sex 1.2 times per week, or just about five times a month.[18] Furthermore, according to a study of more than 30,000 couples, those who had sex once a week reported the greatest levels of satisfaction in their marriages. Thus, in general, frequent sex does help increase happiness. But before you highlight this in yellow and race off to show your spouse, the researchers also found that "daily" isn't necessary. Anything above once a week didn't show a significant rise in happiness.[19] Sorry! If you both honestly feel satisfied with the frequency of your sexual intimacy, then it's a healthy sex life for you. As one expert explains:

> Each person's sex drive is different, each couple's marriage is different, and their daily lives are different. Since there are so many factors at play, it's really hard to know what is "normal." The better question to ask is, what is normal for you and your spouse? Or what would each of you like your "normal" to be?[20]

The bottom line is that there really is no magic number for how often a couple should be having sex. But we really like the above question, "What would each of you like your 'normal' to be?" So, let's talk specifically about how to resurrect a sexless marriage.

We believe the Old Testament book of Hosea has amazing application for your sex life. The first chapter and a half of Hosea is focused on God's anger toward His unfaithful bride, the people of Israel. God told Hosea to marry a promiscuous woman and have children with her to illustrate the way Israel had forsaken God by worshiping other gods. God is clearly angry. He doesn't want to forgive His bride. He wants to punish her by withholding love.

But then midway through chapter two, something remarkable happens. Instead of punishing His adulterous bride, God makes a dramatic shift and outlines a plan to win her back. God allures His bride through tenderness. Notice how God's heart softens. He goes from anger and judgment to gentleness.

You may feel angry or humiliated for being rejected sexually by your spouse. Maybe sex has always been absent in your marriage. Instead of punishing your spouse, reach out in tender compassion. But tender compassion will only happen if your heart is *open*.

1. Soften Your Heart

Rekindling your sexual intimacy begins with a tender, open heart. Ask your heavenly Father to replace your closed or hardened heart with a heart of flesh toward your spouse. Since emotions are the voice of your heart, talk to God about your feelings. Think about your sexual relationship. Maybe you've felt . . .

- *Rejected* as you've initiated sex only to be refused
- *Manipulated* or *pressured* to be intimate
- *Criticized* for your performance
- *Unwanted* or *not pretty enough*
- *Compared* to an ex-spouse
- *Judged* for being too tired or exhausted
- *Embarrassed* about performance issues
- *Ugly* because you've gained weight and your spouse doesn't seem to be attracted to you
- *Humiliated* when asked to do something you weren't comfortable doing
- *Unloved* by your spouse's self-interest
- *Guilty* for how you've treated your spouse
- *Ashamed* for being unfaithful or for introducing pornography into your marriage

It might be something else entirely. Pray like King David, "Search me, O God, and know my heart! Try me and know my thoughts!" (Psalm 139:23). It's amazing what happens to your heart when you pinpoint the specific painful emotion. Speaking it out loud or writing it down has a powerful effect. The clarity allows your heart to become tender.

As your heart softens, finish praying David's words: "See if there be any grievous way in me, and lead me in the way everlasting!" (Psalm 139:24). Sexual difficulties are rarely one-sided. Ask God to give you insight into your part of the problem. You can't change your spouse, but you can deal with your side. Maybe you've acted with self-interest, control, manipulation, indifference, unresponsiveness, or in uncaring ways. What is your part? Ask your spouse for forgiveness. And offer forgiveness to your spouse as well.

Finally, ask God for His eyes and His truth to see your spouse anew. Satan is so cunning. As the "father of lies," he wants to deceive you. He wants you to believe untruths about your spouse and your marriage that are distorted or aren't true. *My husband will always try to control me in bed. My wife will never pursue me sexually.* Pray for God's truth about your spouse.

2. Uncover the Real Issues

As God modeled, speaking tenderly is about opening hearts for real connection. Once your heart is open, you have an opportunity to talk about the real issue from a place of gentleness and compassion.

A lack of sexual initiation or responsiveness is usually a symptom of a deeper problem. If sex is missing from your marriage, discover why. If you don't want sex, investigate what's going on for you. If sex has always been absent, what has contributed to the avoidance of intimacy? What issues pertain to you and your marriage?

The only way to restore your sexual relationship is to get to the root of the problem. However, when sex disappears in a marriage, it's easy to misattribute you spouse's little or no interest in sex to a porn addiction, infidelity, misaligned priorities, fondness for an ex-spouse, same-sex attraction, or lack of attraction. But, in reality, there are many reasons for a sexless marriage. Here are the most common reasons for sexual problems in a marriage. As you read through the list, focus on yourself. Don't make this about your spouse—that's his or her job.

- Health problems such as low thyroid, low testosterone, arthritis, diabetes, high blood pressure, heart disease, or cancer[21]

- Performance-related problems such as premature ejaculation, erectile dysfunction, painful intercourse (dyspareunia) or a disability[22]

- Medication side effects (e.g., antidepressants, birth control pills, over-the-counter antihistamines, anti-seizure drugs)

- Alcohol and drug use

- Temporary circumstances such as childbirth, job loss, bereavement

- Technology (TVs, laptops, or cell phones) in the bedroom

- Exhaustion from caring for young children, a child with special needs, or aging parents

- Fear of pregnancy

- Negative associations about sex (i.e., sex is dirty or sinful, how you were treated by an ex-spouse)

- Hormone changes (e.g., pregnancy, breastfeeding, menopause)

- Sex isn't enjoyable (i.e., painful or uncomfortable intercourse, never orgasm)

- Mental health issues such as anxiety or depression

- Excessive stress (e.g., financial, work, childcare)

- Poor body image and low self-esteem

- History of sexual abuse, past sexual trauma

- Age-related sexual indifference or decreased sexual activity. Older couples are much more likely to be sexually inactive. They are more likely to have health problems, lower energy levels, experience erectile dysfunction and vaginal dryness, and have decreased testosterone and estrogen.[23]

- Predictability or boredom in your sexual relationship

- Low libido (sex drive) or seasons when one spouse is temporarily uninterested

- Sexually acting out (e.g., infidelity, excessive masturbation) or the use of pornography. Several recent studies have revealed that an increase in erectile dysfunction in younger men may be related to pornography use.[24]

- Relationship challenges such as unresolved conflict, resentment about the division of household chores and childcare, neglect, lack of emotional connection, poor communication, trust issues, poor hygiene, not being attracted to your spouse, or withholding sex.

- Sleeping in separate beds or rooms because of quirks such as snoring, nocturnal TV-watching, restless sleep, thermostat wars, one is a bed or blanket "hog," early morning work schedule, etc. One study found that as many as 40 percent of couples will sleep in different beds or rooms at some point.[25]

We know this is a long list. But you're searching for the deeper issues and accuracy is important. What's been going on with you that has contributed to the avoidance of sexual intimacy?

We went through a frustrating season within our sexual relationship. We had been married for a few years and Greg was in graduate school. I (Erin) always assumed that as the guy, Greg would pursue me sexually. Thus, I was confused when I realized that it had been a while since we'd had sex. That night, I put on my sexiest lingerie and waited for Greg to finish studying. When Greg slipped into bed, I snuggled up next to him and waited expectantly. And waited . . . and waited . . . nothing!

"Is everything okay?" I questioned.

"Sure," he replied quickly. "I'm fine. Why?"

"Why are you ignoring me?" I asked feeling rejected.

"I'm not ignoring you," Greg defended. "I'm just really tired. Can we try in the morning?"

"Can we *try* tomorrow?" I echoed sarcastically. "Whatever!"

We both laid there in silence. The next morning Greg was gone when I awoke. *I guess we're not trying tomorrow*, I thought to myself. I felt so hurt and rejected. My mind quickly jumped to several negative conclusions. Was he interested in a classmate? Was he into porn? After giving birth to our daughter, was I no longer attractive to him?

It took a few days before our hearts were open enough to talk. I'd be lying if I said that the conversation started off right. We instantly jumped into our typical conflict patterns. I attacked and blamed. Greg defended and withdrew. But we took a short break to calm down and ended up having a really productive talk about the real issue.

"I don't want to argue," I interrupted Greg's defensiveness. "I really want to listen and better understand what is really going on for you. Let me start over."

Greg hesitantly shook his head in agreement.

"I've noticed that we haven't been intimate in several months." I gently stated, "I've jumped to conclusions about *why*. But, instead of me guessing, I'd like to better understand why you haven't seemed interested in sex lately."

Greg shared that he was really stressed out from school. His comprehensive exams were quickly approaching and he wasn't feeling confident that he would pass. He was struggling with fear about failing and not graduating. Greg also shared that he had been comfort eating to deal with the stress and had put on some extra weight.

It's amazing how quickly my heart softened toward Greg when I understood the deeper issue that he was struggling with. I was also quickly moved to compassion for how he was feeling and the fear that he was experiencing.

I was also able to share the rejection that I was feeling and how his uninterest made me question my attractiveness and his faithfulness. Greg did a great job of validating my hurt and confusion.

Our gentle conversation about the real issues took us to a place of deep connection and intimacy. Although it took some time, we were able to get our sexual relationship back on track in a way that felt good to both of us.

What about you? What issues affect you? If it's a health problem, hormone change, or a medication side effect, go see your doctor. If it's an addiction (e.g., porn, drugs, alcohol), mental health, or an emotional challenge such as past sexual trauma, fear of pregnancy, low self-esteem, or a negative association about sex, then get help from a Christian counselor or treatment center. If it's exhaustion or a temporary circumstance, then verbally acknowledge this season so your spouse doesn't take it personally. You may need to rid your master bedroom of technology including TVs, laptops, or smartphones. If you're sleeping in separate beds or rooms because of snoring or work schedules, start off in the same bed so you can connect emotionally and sexually and then move to a separate bed.

Instead of guessing or jumping to conclusions about why your spouse isn't interested in sex, ask. But this conversation needs to feel safe for both people. An authentic talk about such an emotionally charged topic will only happen if hearts stay open. Blame, defensiveness, withdrawal, or anger will quickly derail the discussion. Never talk about your sexual relationship while trying to have sex or right after sex. You don't want to blindside your spouse. Instead, pick a neutral time and let your spouse know that you'd like to talk about your intimacy. Say something like, "I know we've had a difficult time talking about our sexual relationship. In past attempts, you may have felt blamed, attacked, or ignored. And for that I'm sorry. I don't want to argue about who's right or who's wrong, or debate who's at fault. Instead, I want to talk about what's really going on. Like an iceberg, we've argued about the surface problems like how often we should be having sex or how to spice things up. But I'd really like to go below the surface and figure out what's at the core for both of us. But I want this to be a safe conversation. Is this something that you'd be willing to do?"

3. Restore Your Sexual Relationship

After alluring her with tenderness, God then *restores* the relationship with His bride. "And there I will give her her vineyards and make the Valley of Achor a door of hope. And there she shall answer as in the days of her youth, as at the time when she came out of the land of Egypt" (Hosea 2:15).

Restore means to "return something that was taken away."[26] God is restoring what He removed from their relationship. When God was punishing His bride for her unfaithfulness, He removed what was most precious to her. "And I will lay waste her vines and her fig trees, of which she said, 'These are my wages, which my lovers have given me.'" (Hosea 2:12). But now, God is restoring what was taken away.

What do you need to restore within your relationship? What have you been withholding? Perhaps it's affection, romance, kissing, foreplay, intercourse, fidelity, playfulness, understanding, flirtation, patience, pursuit, curiosity, date nights, desire, compassion, purity, respect, priority, pleasure, attention, or initiation. Maybe you need to restore your interest in sex or your ability to have sex by taking good care of yourself physically, mentally, and emotionally.

God also restores His bride's *hope*. This is significant because the Israelites would have associated the Valley of Achor with disgrace and punishment.[27] But God is telling His bride that He is restoring this dishonorable place that has represented pain. Instead of despair, the valley will now represent *hope*.

A sexless marriage is often the culmination of many painful experiences and bad memories. It's easy to remember feeling rejected, manipulated, or betrayed. The feelings of being unwanted, ugly, or not good enough are difficult to forget. It may be the painful memories tied to an ex-spouse. Time doesn't simply heal the shame of being forced to do something uncomfortable or being humiliated. Reclaim these painful memories. Turn them into signs of hope. A ritual is a powerful way to facilitate this type of healing. Like when dedicating a new house, we encourage you to write Scripture verses throughout your master bedroom, behind your headboard and on your bedposts to re-establish Christ as the cornerstone of your marriage and sexual relationship. Here are some of our favorite verses to purify your memories and reclaim hope in your bedroom:

Whatever house you enter, first say, "Peace be to this house!" (Luke 10:5)

Because you have made the Lord your dwelling place— the Most High, who is my refuge—no evil shall be allowed to befall you, no plague come near your tent. (Psalm 91:9-10)

By wisdom a house is built, and by understanding it is established; by knowledge the rooms are filled with all precious and pleasant riches. (Proverbs 24:3-4)

For you, O Lord God, have spoken, and with your blessing shall the house of your servant be blessed forever. (2 Samuel 7:29)

But as for me and my house, we will serve the Lord. (Joshua 24:15)

Restoring hope happens as you reclaim these memories and past experiences. But the pain and trauma may have been so severe that you need to seek counseling. A good Christian counselor can help you heal from painful memories and reclaim these for good moving forward. Focus on the Family has an excellent Christian counselor referral network that you can search by location or specialty (www.ChristianCounselors.network).

4. Renew Your Sexual Relationship

In Hosea 2:19-20, God says to His bride, "And I will betroth you to me forever. I will betroth you to me in righteousness and in justice, in steadfast love and in mercy. I will betroth you to me in faithfulness." Three times God uses the word *betroth*. He is renewing their relationship by going back to the beginning of their marriage—all the way to their engagement. He's saying, "Let's start over and build a new relationship based on core values like righteousness, justice, steadfast love, mercy, and faithfulness."

What will be the foundation of your new sexual relationship? If pornography, infidelity, or painful memories tied to an ex-spouse have damaged your marriage, this is your opportunity to build a new foundation. What are some important values that you want to build into your lovemaking? Things such as purity, communication, faithfulness, playfulness, honesty, curiosity, integrity, mutual enjoyment, grace, understanding, and compassion. Talk about what is most important for you both and build that into your renewed sexual relationship.

As a husband, maybe you need to renew how you pursue your wife inside and outside the bedroom. Notice how God designed the male body for sex. The way a man's body was created implies "initiation." By God's perfect design, physiologically, before sex is even possible, the man must initiate an erection. The word *erect* means to create, establish, or build something.[28] In the same way that a man must become erect before entering his wife sexually, he should first initiate wooing her. If you want your wife to be more interested in sex, become "interesting" outside the bedroom. If she seems indifferent or unresponsive to your sexual advances, then become attractive nonsexually.

Allure your wife by connecting with her emotionally—go after her heart and soul. For example, your wife may also be feeling overwhelmed from carrying too many responsibilities with too little help and appreciation from you. Don't get defensive and say, "I have a lot on my plate as well!" Ask her if she feels alone regarding childcare and household responsibilities. A recent *New York Post* headline read, "Wanna have more sex? Do the dishes." Research shows that couples who evenly share household chores have more sex than couples where the woman does the bulk of the housework.[29] When chores and childcare are divided equally, a wife feels a greater sense of being honored and cherished, and this often leads to more intimacy.

However, we're not suggesting that this is a "guaranteed" formula: *Woo your wife outside the bedroom and she will respond sexually in the bedroom.* Marriage doesn't work that way. More importantly, pursuing your wife nonsexually is about living out God's call to love her unconditionally and sacrificially (Ephesians 5:25) and not because it might increase your chances in the bedroom. Never pressure your wife to have sex or use God's Word to force sex. No must be an acceptable response. If no isn't an option, then you're not making a request; you're making a demand and that isn't who God is calling you to be as a husband.

Husbands, in the bedroom make your goal *mutual* enjoyment. Sex isn't just about you climaxing—it's not just about you! Woo your wife sexually by making her sexual desires and satisfaction matter just as much as yours—both need to matter. Prioritize and "initiate" sexual experiences that matter to your wife: Massage her body, whisper that she's beautiful and sexy, slow down the foreplay, make sure she climaxes, and end with cuddling and pillow talk. This helps her feel like a soulmate—someone who is valued and not objectified. If you're not sure what your wife likes sexually, we have some great questions for you to ask her at the end of this chapter!

As the wife, if your husband's body was made to initiate, the female body was made to open and receive her husband. By God's perfect design, physiologically, a man's erect penis is received by the open wife. You can't control whether your husband initiates or how he initiates, but you can control being open and able to receive from your husband. *Receive* means "accept" or "welcome."[30] Availability then is about proactively preparing yourself emotionally, spiritually, mentally, and physically to receive your husband.

However, when women hear advice like "reserve some energy for your husband so you're not so tired when he wants you sexually," "initiate sex periodically," and "respond more often," it can feel as if *he* is the only one who matters, as if wives are just objects for their husband's enjoyment. When we use the words "receive" or "welcome" when your husband initiates sex (bid for connection), we aren't suggesting that you make it just about his sexual needs. God gave your marriage the gift of sex for *both* of you to enjoy. Respond sexually to bless your husband and your marriage, but also because *you* get to enjoy it as well. Your sexual experience isn't less important than his—*you* matter! *Both* people need to matter!

How can you renew your availability in the bedroom? I (Erin) always have a choice as to how I will respond to Greg and how I show up within the sexual component of our marriage. Honestly, I don't want to feel like sex is merely a duty, a chore, or an obligation. We need to celebrate and delight in the act of sex with our spouse with the goal of *mutual* enjoyment. Certainly sex can bond us emotionally, but sometimes we need to physically connect before we can emotionally connect. I (Erin) often tell young wives, "Win your husband's body to win his heart." Emotional connection is intensified when you physically *yada* (know) your husband and experience sex in ways that both people enjoy.

As a couple, think about the way things were when you were newly married. What was different about that season? Maybe you prioritized date nights, romance was in the air, you took showers together, you had good bedroom manners (no toe nail clippings or passing gas) and personal hygiene, you lingered in bed, you came to bed early, you didn't watch TV in bed or didn't charge your cell phone next to the bed, foreplay lasted longer than several minutes, or you took long walks where you talked about your inner lives. We know that the demands of work, childcare, and household responsibilities make it almost impossible to go back to these early years. But talk about what was different back then and see if there are specific things that you can recreate.

Another aspect of renewing your sexual relationship is to prioritize communication. One hallmark of a sexless marriage is the couple avoids talking about sex. As a married couple, you need to feel safe to discuss your sexual relationship together—to talk honestly and openly about your own sexual likes and dislikes. However, we would encourage you to find a neutral time to talk—not right before or right after sex. Here are some of our favorite sex conversation starters.

- What is the best way to "flirt" (e.g., texting, email, phone call, notes, words, actions)? Describe what flirting looks like to you.
- Describe your ideal nonsexual physical affection (e.g., holding hands, hugs, kissing, shoulder massages, back rubs, cuddling, spooning) and how often you desire it.
- How do you like to be romanced during the day in anticipation of sex?
- Is connecting emotionally before we have sex important to you? If so, how would you like to connect?
- What do you remember about the first time we had sex?
- On a scale of 1-10, how strong is your sex drive? Is it increasing or is it diminishing?
- Given your current sex drive, how often would you like to have sex?
- Describe the perfect evening of lovemaking?
- How could our sex life become even better?
- What do I wear that puts you in the mood?
- Do you have a favorite sex position? Why is it your favorite?
- What turns you off sexually? Is there anything sexually you find wrong, offensive, or distasteful?
- Sexually, do you prefer me to make the first move or do you like to do it?

- What do I do that gives you the most sexual pleasure?
- What do you fantasize about? What kind of fantasizing is okay with you?
- What do you do to show me that you are interested in having sex?
- What are your favorite foreplay activities?
- Where are some places you would like to have sex outside of our bedroom?
- What do you like to do right after making love?

Great sex requires regular communication. Enjoy rediscovering the sexual side of your spouse!

Hosea 2:20 ends with God saying, "And you shall know the LORD." When God says to His wife, "you shall *know* the Lord . . ." He is talking about the word, *yada*, as in an intimate relationship. God is promising to withhold nothing from His bride, and she will deeply know (*yada*) Him!

Don't let *Seinfeld*, or anyone for that matter, hijack your "yada, yada, yada" and turn it into something other than what God intended. God's idea of *yada* is for you to know your spouse completely, be deeply known by your spouse, and to enjoy each other sexually. Recognize that God gave you the amazing gift of sex. Decide together what "normal" means for you in the bedroom. Discuss your needs openly with your spouse and negotiate a sexual relationship that meets your needs in a way that feels good to both of you. Be patient. Reviving your sexual relationship will take time so celebrate small victories. *Yada* is a powerful gift for your marriage, so guard and protect it well.

Roommates rarely have sex;

soulmates have sex often in a way

that feels good to both people.

CHAPTER 11

The Closed Heart

Love one another deeply from the heart.

1 PETER 1:22, NIV

Roommates allow their love to grow cold;

soulmates keep their hearts open and create a marriage

that feels like the safest place on earth.

Once Bitten, Twice Shy

In the popular ad campaign for her jewelry line, actor and business-woman Jane Seymour declares, "If your heart is open, love will always find its way in."

Cheesy? Undeniably. Her famous quote is dripping with mushiness.

Profound? Absolutely. Next to our relationship with Jesus Christ, keeping your heart open is the most significant relationship truth we've learned. A soulmate marriage is only possible when hearts are fully open to each other. It's exactly what the apostle Paul was saying to the Corinthian Christians: "Oh, my dear Corinthian friends! I have told you all my feelings; I love you with all my heart. Any coldness still between us is not because of any lack of love on my part but because your love is too small and does not reach out to me and draw me in. I am talking to you now as if you truly were my very own children. Open your hearts to us! Return our love!" (2 Corinthians 6:11-13, TLB).

161

Open your hearts. This is a wonderful poetic notion, but it's much easier said than done. Many people struggle with keeping their heart open because openness requires vulnerability, as Drs. Arch Hart and Sharon Hart May explain:

> When a husband and wife love each other, they literally
> give their hearts to each other for safekeeping. This is such a
> delicate, trusting act that any violation or injury of this trust
> can cause the most painful of reactions. Imagine taking the
> very essence of your being—your heart—and placing it in the
> hands of your spouse. Your heart becomes your mate's to care
> for, safe-guard, cherish, and love. This necessitates a willingness
> to be vulnerable and take a bold, risky step."[1]

This is the ultimate dilemma in marriage: In order to reach the most profound levels of connection, you have to give your spouse access to the most vulnerable part of you—your heart. The risk is there's no guarantee how he or she will handle your heart. Once open, will you be unconditionally loved and accepted? After seeing the real you—all of your flaws, imperfections, embarrassing stories, and past mistakes—will you be cherished and protected?

We long to be unconditionally loved and accepted. But many people enter into marriage already afraid of being open and vulnerable. As young children, we quickly learn that the world is full of pain and heartache. We all have emotional bruises and relationship scars from the past. We've placed our trust in people who've hurt us. Maybe your childhood included abuse in all its insidious forms. Perhaps you watched your parents divorce. Maybe you had a bad experience in a previous dating relationship. Perhaps a best friend unexpectedly ended your friendship. Maybe you were physically or sexually assaulted. Perhaps you were married before. Maybe you made a mistake and believe it's unforgiveable. Traumatic experiences only reinforce that people and/or relationships

aren't safe. This collective damage causes us to come up with a whole host of strategies to avoid intimacy and keep from being hurt. Consider these defenses:

- Build emotional walls
- Maintain shallow relationships
- Use humor to distract people from seeing the real person
- Veg out in front of the TV or computer
- Spend countless hours on social media or playing video games
- Use anger to control others from getting too close
- Overly invest in children, work, or hobbies
- Exist in a sexless marriage
- Turn to food for comfort
- Prioritize time with friends
- Project certain personas on social media
- Don't talk about feelings
- Isolate and hide out in a man cave or she-shed
- Anesthetize pain through addictions
- Get involved in an affair
- Become self-reliant to avoid depending on anyone
- Disappear when people get too close

Unfortunately, the strategies we use to keep from being hurt are self-defeating because they require significant energy and severely impact the intimacy in your marriage. It's hard for your spouse to get close when you're on the other side of a thick wall.

This keeps us stuck in a roommate marriage.

Others want to open their heart and deeply connect with their spouse, but the relationship feels unsafe. It's like the insurance salesman explained to his customer: "Your application was filled out correctly except for one thing, Mr. Smith. Where it asks the relationship of Mrs. Smith to yourself, you should have put down *wife*, not *strained*."

It's difficult to open your heart when your marriage feels strained and you constantly feel like you're walking on eggshells around your spouse. Instead of your marriage feeling like a safe haven, you feel apprehensive or stressed being around your spouse.

While there are probably hundreds of ways to offend, frustrate, and hurt each other—causing our hearts to shut down—we consistently see several that top the list. Trying to better understand why people close their hearts, we asked hundreds of couples to answer the question: "What causes you to feel *unsafe* in your marriage?" Here are the top responses and the behaviors that make a marriage feel unsafe:

- Being criticized (this was number one)
- Being physically threatened, intimidated, or abused
- Feeling put down or belittled
- When your spouse emotionally withdraws
- When hurtful jokes or sarcastic comments are at your expense
- Having your feelings, thoughts, beliefs, and opinions judged
- Being ignored or minimized
- Feeling controlled
- Being verbally attacked
- When your spouse intensely defends himself/herself
- Being yelled at or spoken to with harsh words
- When promises are broken
- Being incessantly nagged
- When your spouse shares private information without your permission
- Having past mistakes repeatedly brought up
- When your spouse doesn't listen
- Feeling unloved, rejected, or abandoned
- When you don't get the benefit of the doubt
- Being deceived
- Feeling disrespected

- Being embarrassed or humiliated in front of others
- Suffering a betrayal or infidelity
- When affection or sex is withheld or used as a weapon
- Feeling like your opinion doesn't matter
- When your spouse is unwilling to admit he or she is wrong or seek forgiveness
- Being forced to do something that you're uncomfortable with
- When your spouse tries to "fix" you
- When your needs are dismissed as unimportant

It might be something obvious from the above list, or it might be something subtle like tone of voice, a certain negative look, a shake of the head, or rolling of the eyes, but when we encounter these wrongs, we feel *unsafe* and instantly go into "fight or flight" mode—we counterattack or withdraw. So, how can you tell that a heart has closed? Here are some signs that a heart has shut down:

- Little or no eye contact
- Negative body language (i.e., folded or crossed arms, glaring, pouting)
- Silence or withdrawal—disconnecting relationally or physically leaving the room
- Bitterness and resentment
- Anger (e.g., yelling, intimidation)
- Harshness or acting cruel
- Refusing touch
- Insensitivity or callousness
- Selfishness
- Unwillingness to forgive
- Emotional distance or coldness
- Despair and hopelessness

A closed heart makes us dangerous relationally. When my heart is closed and I (Erin) become critical, I'm really not a safe person to be around. Not only am I likely to say or do something that will hurt my husband, I'm also unsafe because I'm consumed with *me*. I'm trying to get rid of *my* hurtful feelings, and I'm not really thinking about Greg. I've lost perspective. When a turtle's head is retracted or a roly-poly bug is curled up tight, it can't see beyond itself. The world around becomes dark. King David spoke about not being able to see when his heart was troubled: "For evils have encompassed me beyond number; my iniquities have overtaken me, and I cannot see; they are more than the hairs of my head; my heart fails me" (Psalm 40:12).

When our hearts shut down we become confused. Our judgment is clouded. Awareness, insight, and discernment are nonexistent. In this closed state we often end up making brain-only decisions that are heartless. It's so easy to rationalize our choices when we lack perspective and are just using our brain. This is why good people are capable of making terrible choices when their hearts are shut. We've all heard someone say, "He was the last person on earth I thought would do that," or "I never thought she was capable of doing that." We become capable of practically anything when our hearts are closed. And the longer our hearts remain closed, the more likely our hearts are going to fossilize or *harden*.

One of the things that we've learned over the years of working with marriages that are in crisis is that every failed relationship stems from a *hardened heart*. A hardened heart is the real destroyer of our marriages. Max Lucado agrees: "A hard heart ruins, not only your life, but the lives of your family members. As an example, Jesus identified the hard heart as the wrecking ball of a marriage."[2] In Matthew 19:8, Jesus talks about divorce in the context of a hardened heart, and He goes on to explain that this wasn't God's original plan. Jesus said, "Because of your hardness of heart Moses allowed you to divorce your wives, but from the beginning it was not so."

The good news is that closed hearts can open and hardened hearts can soften over time. But it starts with *your* heart.

Healing Your Heart

You will never move from roommates to soulmates in your marriage if your heart is closed or hardened. It's exactly as the Tin Man from *The Wizard of Oz* came to realize: "It was a terrible thing to undergo, but during the year I stood there I had time to think that the greatest loss I had known was the loss of my heart. While I was in love, I was the happiest man on earth; but no one can love who has not a heart, and so I am resolved to ask Oz to give me one."[3]

Healing your heart doesn't require you to follow the yellow brick road in search of Oz the Great and Powerful Wizard. Your heart is healed by the God who heals the brokenhearted and binds up their wounds (Psalm 147:3).

First, notice the state of your heart toward your spouse. Is your heart open or closed? If your heart is closed to whatever degree, don't judge yourself. Self-judgment will make you feel worse, and your emotional walls will grow higher and thicker. Instead of self-condemnation, be curious: "I wonder why my heart is closed?" Earlier we suggested that it could be because you either walked into marriage with emotional walls based on early traumatic experiences or you don't feel safe in your marriage.

If you walked into your marriage with emotional walls, do something about it. The state of your heart is *your* responsibility. In Proverbs 4:23, King Solomon writes, "Keep vigilant watch over your heart; that's where life starts" (MSG). Solomon is saying that your heart is the wellspring of God's life-giving love. He isn't saying to guard your heart by hiding it behind a thick wall. He is telling us to keep our heart open. He is imploring us to guard our hearts from closing, or worse, from hardening, because if our hearts are closed, God's love can't spring out of them. Guarding our hearts from closing is our job.

God can heal your heart, no matter the condition. You just need to ask.

"'Yet even now,' declares the LORD, 'return to me with all your heart . . . rend your hearts and not your garments. Return to the LORD your God . . .'" (Joel 2:12-13). This is an amazing passage of Scripture. To rend something is to tear or split it into pieces. Throughout the Bible, there are many examples of people deliberately tearing their clothing as a physical expression of grief—they were literally saying, "it tears me up."[4] In this verse, instead of our clothes, we are being told to tear our hearts in order that we might return to the Lord.

Ask God to heal your heart. He is so faithful. But there are times when a broken bone can only heal when it is rebroken. Likewise, your heart must be cracked open to allow God's healing love to penetrate. The opportunity is to rend open your heart so the Lord can perform a miracle. He makes this promise: "I will sprinkle clean water on you, and you shall be clean from all your uncleannesses, and from all your idols I will cleanse you. And I will give you a new heart" (Ezekiel 36:25-26).

You don't have to live with a closed or hardened heart. God will heal your heart if you ask. A softened, open heart is all God needs to begin moving you from a roommate to a soulmate marriage. If God can raise the dead, He can absolutely resurrect a hardened heart. We've witnessed this miracle countless times!

Creating a Marriage That Feels Like the Safest Place on Earth

As we've mentioned, love is risky and there is no guarantee that we won't get hurt. So, how do we create deep connection with our spouse in spite of the obvious risks? It's important to create the right type of environment so hearts open.

Safety isn't simply a list of behaviors; it's a state of being. Being safe is a way of life. You see, God is passionate about you. He wants a personal relationship with you. After all, He sent His Son to die for you so that you could spend eternity with Him. This is the purest love. And a foundational characteristic of God's love is *safety*. He makes this message clear through the Scriptures:

"The name of the LORD is a strong tower; the righteous man runs into it and is safe." (Proverbs 18:10)

"Save me, O God, because I have come to you for refuge." (Psalm 16:1, TLB)

"In peace I will both lie down and sleep; for you alone, O LORD, make me dwell in safety." (Psalm 4:8)

"The fear of man lays a snare, but whoever trusts in the LORD is safe." (Proverbs 29:25)

These are just a few of the many verses that show the safety we have in God. He wants your heart open so you can receive His everlasting love and so you can love Him wholeheartedly.

We like what John and Stasi Eldredge say about creating a safe marriage.

> Marriage is the sanctuary of the heart. You have been entrusted with the heart of another human being. Whatever else your life's great mission will entail, loving and defending this heart next to you is part of your great quest. Marriage is the privilege and the honor of living as close to the heart as two people can get. No one else in all the world has the opportunity to know each other more intimately than do a husband and wife. We are invited into their secret lives, their truest selves; we come to know their nuances, their particular tastes, what they think is funny, what drives them crazy. We are entrusted with their hopes and dreams, their wounds, and their fears.[5]

So what is emotional safety? We define emotional safety as feeling free to open your heart and be fully known and know that your spouse will unconditionally love, accept, protect, nourish, and cherish you as an imperfect person.

So, how do we pull this off? How do we create a marriage that feels like the safest place on earth? We asked couples at our marriage seminar to define emotional safety. Listen to some of their responses:

- Feeling secure—a deep sense that our relationship is unbreakable
- Being loved unconditionally and accepted for who I am
- Feeling relaxed and peaceful
- Being cared for above anyone else
- Being fully known—to see me for who I am
- Being free to express who I really am
- Feeling respected
- Feeling valued and cherished
- Not being judged
- Accepting my flaws as part of the whole package

That's a pretty amazing list, isn't it? Wouldn't it feel wonderful to have these things as the foundation of your marital relationship?

When your spouse feels safe, she is naturally inclined to relax and open her heart. In this open state, connection occurs effortlessly. You don't have to force closeness or do things to create intimacy when you feel safe. It takes much more effort and energy to stay closed or locked behind an emotional wall. Think about a recent time when your spouse hurt or frustrated you. Do you remember how quickly your heart closed and how you disconnected from your spouse? Your heart was not designed to stay closed. Maintaining a closed heart is like trying to force a huge beach ball under water. You have to strain and push to keep a ball full of air under the water. You have to work really hard to keep a heart full of God's love shut down. Have you ever noticed that when your spouse takes responsibility for his or her actions and seeks forgiveness, how quickly your heart opens again? Like that beach ball under the water, once you feel safe, your heart will explode back open. You can go from feeling closed to instantly feeling open and connected.

We'll say it one more time: In order for closeness and deep connection to occur, hearts must be open. Thus, the foundation of a soulmate marriage is feeling safe—physically, intellectually, spiritually, and emotionally. So, how do we practically build a marriage that feels like the safest place on earth? It's easier than you may think.

Creating Safety in Your Marriage

We love these characteristics of God: gracious, merciful, slow to anger, and abounding in love (Joel 2:12-13). These aren't just behaviors; these traits define who God is—His way of living. In marriage, there will be no shortage of opportunities to extend these behaviors to your spouse.

Recently I (Greg) was helping Erin cook a family meal. My job was to cook the gluten-free, breaded chicken. I was using Erin's favorite cookware: a skillet and glass lid that she's had for years. After the chicken was a savory golden-brown, I removed the skillet and lid from the stove and placed them both in the sink.

Immediately, from across the kitchen, Erin yelled, "Make sure that you don't run cold water over the lid!"

I'm not an idiot, I thought to myself. *I know how to wash dishes without instructions!*

And then everything went chaotic. One moment I'm rolling my eyes at Erin's nerve in telling me how to clean up, and the next thing I know I've just been shot.

As soon as I ran cold water (yep, that's what I did) over the hot glass lid, the entire thing exploded. All I remember is hearing a loud popping sound and then glass raining down everywhere. It sounded like gunfire, but instead of diving to the ground, I just froze. I stood there like a moron, staring in disbelief at the carnage. All that was left was a handle (which I was still holding) and a 12-inch metal ring rolling to a stop at the bottom of the sink.

I looked at Erin, who now had her hands on her hips, shaking her head.

"I don't think you're supposed to use cold water," I said with a sheepish grin.

So, how do we create safety in the midst of our marital frustrations like we experienced cooking together? Let's unpack these four attributes of God found in Joel 2:12-13 and see how they create safety.

1. Safety Is Slow to Anger. "Return to the LORD your God, for he is . . . slow to anger." The phrase "slow to anger" appears no less than fourteen times throughout Scripture. Being slow to anger means being long-suffering. And long-suffering means exercising "patience"—patience with difficult people. After twenty-seven years of marriage, we understand the importance of patience. It's easy to be hurt, become annoyed, or get frustrated by your spouse. Part of Erin's loving response after my destroying her cookware was patience. Instead of reacting to my blunder, she was slow to anger.

Patience is the capacity to accept or tolerate irritations, delays, problems, or suffering without becoming annoyed or anxious.[6] Think of the countless irritations we face within marriage: Waiting for her to finish getting dressed when you're already fifteen minutes late. His dirty socks on the floor. House lights left on all night long. Late fees from unpaid bills. Snoring. Checking the cell phone while spending time together. The toilet seat left up. Papers and mail piled on the kitchen counter. Thermostat battles. Burping or passing gas. An empty gas tank after borrowing your car. Eating your food without asking.

Patience is giving your spouse the freedom to be human. But, there is a caveat. How do we discern what behaviors to tolerate and which issues to confront? Proverbs 19:11 says, "Smart people know how to hold their tongue; their grandeur is to forgive and forget" (MSG). In marriage, patience includes being able to discern between what God expects and our own desires and expectations. We really like Ashleigh Slater's perspective on patience in marriage:

> So we ask ourselves: Is this behavior missing God's mark? Or is it simply missing mine? Is it a quirk I find grating, or is it offensive to God and hurtful to our relationship? If it's a matter of annoyance, not destructiveness, then we choose to let it go. Sometimes the bothersome things simply aren't worth the battle. Often when we choose to move a bothersome thing to the conversational front burner, it doesn't improve our marriage, it simply feeds one of our needs to have things a certain way.[7]

This is what King Solomon was driving at in Proverbs 19:11. Wisdom knows when to pick a battle and when to let something go. If our spouse's behavior is in direct violation of God's Word or if it is harmful to us personally or to our marriage, then it's worth confronting. Although annoying at times, Erin's propensity to be late isn't missing God's mark. Likewise, as an introvert, Greg's frequent resistance to leaving the house is irritating, but it's not a violation of God's Word. Blowing up my favorite cookware, although frustrating, isn't a battle that needs to be fought. These annoyances fall under the banner of "giving your spouse the freedom to be human."

Patience also includes discerning when to confront destructive patterns for the good of your marriage. Behaviors such as domestic violence, pornography, infidelity, addiction, criminal conduct, unrighteous anger—these behaviors should not be tolerated. Patience with destructive behaviors means that we love the person but hate the sin. It doesn't mean that we tolerate issues that are harming the individual or the marriage. When these types of destructive behaviors are present, patience means that you set a clear boundary. A loving, God-honoring boundary is something that you put in place that keeps your heart *open* to your spouse. We encourage you to meet with a Christian counselor to help you think through what a godly boundary might look like within your specific situation.

2. Safety Is Gracious. Besides almost being killed by glass cookware, the most amazing part of our story was that Erin didn't say a word. She had every right to be upset and to feel frustrated with me; after all, I had ignored her warning and vaporized her favorite cooking vessel. She would have been justified in lecturing me or demanding that I clean up the mess I'd created.

But she did none of that. Instead, she calmly walked over and inspected my face for shrapnel wounds from the exploding lid and helped me sweep up the 900 tiny pieces of glass that were strewn across the kitchen floor. Why did she respond this way? One word comes to mind: *grace*.

Theologically speaking, grace is an essential way that God expresses His love for us. In fact, the word *grace* is used more than 170 times in the New Testament alone.[8] The *Oxford English Dictionary* defines grace as "the free and unmerited favor of God, as manifested in the salvation of sinners and the bestowal of blessings."[9]

Grace has a way of recalibrating our relationships. It's not that you're ignoring or minimizing serious problems; instead you're deciding how you want to show up in your marriage. Remember, grace is unearned kindness and the bestowing of blessings.

So how can we emulate God and apply this amazing gift within our marriage? In simple terms, extending grace to our spouse means to love him exactly where he is.

Greg isn't perfect. Grace means looking past the things Greg does that frustrate me to see what's true about him. It's about remembering who Greg really is on the inside, not just how he's irritating me in the moment. Grace means believing the best about your spouse. It fights through the messiness of a particular moment or behavior and remembers that your spouse is a son or daughter of the most high King. He or she is made in God's image and is valuable—this is *always* true!

This is exactly what Erin did for me (Greg) after I shattered the glass lid. In that moment, Erin gave me the benefit of the doubt. This is a powerful attribute of grace. Instead of making assumptions about our spouse's motives, grace tries to understand where he or she is coming from. Giving the benefit of the doubt forces us to then check out the truth: "I know your heart even though your present actions are perplexing. Help me understand what's going on."

Instead of demanding a "pound of flesh," Erin lived out Ephesians 4:32: "Be kind to one another, tenderhearted, forgiving one another, as God in Christ forgave you."

3. Safety Is Merciful. Another word for merciful is compassionate.[10] According to the Wikipedia online encyclopedia, compassion is defined as a "profound human emotion prompted by the pain of others. More vigorous than empathy, the feeling commonly gives rise to an active desire to alleviate another's suffering."[11]

Compassion is caring about our spouse's feelings. "Put on then, as God's chosen ones, holy and beloved, compassionate hearts, kindness, humility, meekness, and patience" (Colossians 3:12). This sets an amazing tone to move deeper into the journey toward connection and intimacy. When Erin is hurting, she doesn't want me to ignore her and pretend nothing is going on. She doesn't want me to say, "Calm down!" She doesn't want me to compare her situation to the less fortunate. Instead, Erin wants me to hurt with her, experience her emotions, feel her pain, put myself in her shoes, and to see things from her perspective. A heart will open when it feels safe. And compassion creates safety.

As we were lying in bed that night, after I (Greg) shattered Erin's prized cookware, I lamented, "That was crazy, right? I could have been seriously injured from all that glass exploding."

"Exactly," Erin said. "That's why I told you not to use cold water."

Feeling the emotional energy intensifying, I tried to calm the situation. "Don't worry," I offered, "I'll buy you a new glass lid."

Nailed it! I thought to myself. *Problem solved!*

"Why does everything with you need a solution or need to be fixed?" Erin responded in frustration. "Why can't you care about how I feel?"

"How *you* feel?" I countered. "I'm the one that could have been blinded by all that flying glass. How about a little compassion?"

"Exactly!" Erin shot back.

The ensuing silence made me wonder if I was missing something important.

Every person reading this book is yelling, "You think?"

Even if you have an amazing answer for a problem, your spouse won't care about your brilliance until he or she knows that you *care*. This is exactly what Jesus modeled after His close friend Lazarus died. When Jesus found Lazarus's family deeply grieving, He took time to be compassionate with the family. John 11:35 simply says, "Jesus wept." This has always fascinated us. Why did Jesus "waste" time weeping with the family members? We expected Him to go right for the solution. To solve the problem of Lazarus's death, Jesus raises him from the dead. We don't know about you, but that is an amazing solution! So, being armed with the world's all-time best solution, why did He first empathize with the family? We wonder if part of His lesson was compassion—the importance of connecting *with* someone's heart. Instead of offering a way to fix Erin's broken lid, I missed the opportunity to be compassionate.

After Erin became silent, I asked what was really bothering her (I assumed that it wasn't the $15 lid).

"You're missing the point of my frustration," Erin explained. "I don't care about the lid. That's an easy fix. I'm annoyed that you didn't accept my influence. I knew that cold water would shatter the lid. But you ignored my warning. I felt disregarded."

Every part of me wanted to defend myself. But thankfully I moved toward compassion.

"You're right," I responded. "I did ignore your warning. I'm sure that didn't feel good. I wouldn't like it either if I'd cautioned you about handling something of mine, only to watch you break it."

"Thank you," Erin responded.

"I'm sorry for ignoring you and breaking your lid," I gently offered.

"It's okay," Erin playfully replied. "You can buy me a new Alessi cooking set that I've been eyeing online."

"Sounds fair," I conceded. "I mean how much could it cost?"

Although we were lying in the dark, I could sense her lips curling up into a Grinch-like evil smile. "It's only $4,500 for the twenty-three-piece set!"

Thankfully she was joking (I hope).

We ended up having a nice conversation that night. I let myself feel what it must have felt like to feel ignored. Holding my wife's hand as we talked in bed created a special type of connection that I'm so grateful to have experienced.

I now get how compassion can create safety in our marriage. When you open your heart to your spouse's feelings, you'll get a kinder response in return. We love *The Message*'s version of Proverbs 25:15: "Patient persistence pierces through indifference; gentle speech breaks down rigid defenses." Care and compassion breaks down opposition and creates two open hearts.

4. Safety Is Abounding in Love. God's heart is overflowing with steadfast love for you. He is lovingly committed to you forever, as He makes clear in Jeremiah 31:3: "I have loved you with an everlasting love." A lifelong commitment of abounding love creates security. When people feel secure that their spouse is lovingly committed for life, they are free to fully and completely open their heart.

When the Bible talks about "one flesh" in marriage, it's about the covenant relationship that a husband and wife make with God. Once we make this lifelong commitment to love, we become "glued" or "joined" to each other. A married couple becomes "one flesh" through sexual union, but it's about more than just sex. One flesh is about a deep emotional attachment—being a connected and united team for life.

One flesh happens when a husband and wife are joined together in a close, inseparable relationship. But commitment is more than just saying that we'll be together forever. *The Message*'s version of Malachi 2:15 says something interesting about commitment: "God, not you, made marriage. His Spirit inhabits even the smallest details of marriage. . . . So guard the spirit of marriage within you." The phrase "so guard the spirit of marriage within you" can have a profound impact on your marriage. Commitment isn't a "one and done" experience—something that you pledge at your wedding but then neglect as you move on to sexier aspects of your relationship, such as sharing a spiritual faith, building communication, resolving conflicts, spending time together, making decisions as a team, and so on. Our commitment is something that we must actively guard.

We define commitment as a passionate pledge in which you decide to be with your spouse for a lifetime and to proactively build a future together. Thinking about this definition, we believe that there are three specific ways to guard the spirit of marriage within you—to protect your commitment.

First, commitment is a decision. A husband and wife must "decide" to love each other for a lifetime. Actually, the word *decide* comes from a root word meaning "to cut."[12] In other words, commitment is a decision to cut off all other options that compete against your marriage. We have removed the word *divorce* from our marriage vocabulary. The concept doesn't exist for us.

When divorce isn't an option, instead of "sweeping problems under the rug," our lifelong commitment forces us to work through problems. We don't want to live out our marriage in misery or dissatisfaction (that is a scary idea), so when we have problems or experience conflict, we work to resolve them. Retreat is easy if the option exists.

Second, commitment is a feeling. We don't believe that commitment is simply about making a decision to stay married for life. We also believe commitment involves passion and emotion. One way the emotional side of commitment can show up is by highly valuing your marriage. Hebrews 13:4 says, "Honor your marriage and its vows" (TLB). Honoring marriage means that we recognize its immense worth. In the past, we could write pages about each other's incredible value, but we never really thought about the worth of our marriage. It wasn't like we avoided this thought; it just never occurred to us to think about it in this way. We recently made a list of what we love about our marriage:

- Pursuing God together
- Challenging me to be a better person
- Having fun and laughing together
- Pursuing shared dreams
- Raising our children together (tag team)
- Sex in a way that feels good to both people
- Knowing someone deeply and being deeply known by another
- Serving together
- Living with my best friend
- Having a helpmate—someone to share life's responsibilities
- Being on a grand adventure together
- Being part of a team
- Feeling safe and secure

What about you? What do you value about your marriage? When you clearly recognize the treasure that is your marriage, this sense of value has a great impact on your commitment. In other words, your heart is fully invested in what you consider valuable.

The final element of commitment involves action. It's not just that you "decide" to stay married (decision) or "like" the relationship (passion), but that you're going to take active steps to maintain a strong marriage. This is what 1 John 3:18 is imploring us to do as well: "Let us not love with words or speech but with actions and in truth" (NIV).

The best action is called "grit." Grit is perseverance for long-term goals despite being confronted by significant obstacles and distractions.[13] In marriage, grit is the commitment to do whatever it takes to stay married for a lifetime. It means pressing on when it'd be easier to give up.

Remember, in order for closeness and deep connection to occur, hearts must be open. This is why the apostle Peter beseeches us to "love one another deeply from the heart" (1 Peter 1:22, NIV). And a heart will open only when it feels safe. Therefore create a relationship that feels like the safest place on earth. Follow God's lead and focus on establishing grace, patience, compassion, and a lifelong commitment in your marriage.

Roommates allow their love to grow cold;

soulmates keep their hearts open and create a marriage

that feels like the safest place on earth.

CHAPTER 12

In Our Wildest Dreams

Life has taught us that love does not consist of gazing at each other,

but in looking outward together in the same direction.

ANTOINE DE SAINT-EXUPÉRY

Roommates have no long-term plans;

soulmates pursue shared dreams together.

I (ERIN) WAS AT A WOMEN'S BIBLE study group one day when the leader asked a fascinating question: "What were your dreams as a young girl?"

I perked up thinking, *Ooh, I love talking about dreams.*

Over the next hour, I learned more about these women than I knew about some of my closest friends. The women talked about their dreams of marrying a farmer; becoming a seamstress, a teacher, or a nurse; and one woman even wanted to be an astronaut.

Through tears and laughter, each woman disclosed her unique journey, recalling the turning points and the circumstances that caused her to walk away from these early aspirations. It was heartbreaking to hear the regrets, sense of failure, frustrations, and disappointments of unrealized dreams. But it was powerful to hear about God's faithfulness and how He placed new desires in their hearts, brought different opportunities, opened new doors, and delivered unexpected blessings to each woman.

As a child, you probably had big dreams as well. When we were young, our dreams had no limitations and the world seemed like a never-ending stream of possibilities. As a young girl, I dreamed of being a flight attendant, the first female NBA star (long before the WNBA), writing books, and someday adopting a child. Greg dreamed about playing football for the Dallas Cowboys, being a pilot, and in college, he wanted to be a lawyer. We were born to dream.

God has planted desires in our hearts and given us unique gifts and talents to carry out *His* purposes here on earth. And then you met your spouse and another set of unique aspirations entered the picture. Your individual dreams then joined with another heart, and you began to dream of the endless possibilities *together*.

Think back to when you were seriously dating or when you got engaged. Most young couples dream wildly with no limits on what they can accomplish together. They dream of what their life will look like—how many children they want, where they will live, what career paths they might pursue, which exotic travel locations they want to visit, and what their fairy-tale wedding will include. But then something happens. For many couples, dreaming ends as the rapid pace of life takes over and responsibilities mount. Almost immediately after the wedding, life gets hectic. We get it. Juggling a marriage, running a household, balancing careers, raising children, and tackling a thousand other challenges, who has time to dream big when you're stuck in survival mode?

Once overwhelming routines and responsibilities take control, our big dreams often get set aside. And sadly, most couples aren't even aware that they have stopped dreaming together. But they begin feeling the distance between their hearts and they start feeling like married roommates. At a recent marriage seminar, we posed this question, "What does dreaming together look like in your marriage?" After the session, couple after couple approached us with tear-stained faces, recognizing that at some point, they too had stopped dreaming. And this is tragic. Dreaming together has a powerful impact on a marriage. Something magical happens when we dream together. It brings a unique depth of closeness and connection. Dreaming together . . .

- Strengthens your commitment. Couples who share a vision of the future *want* to stay together. Dreaming implies that you anticipate a hopeful future together.

- Nurtures your *partnership* and helps you strengthen your unity and teamwork.

- Creates intimacy by allowing you to glimpse into your spouse's heart—their innermost thoughts and feelings.

- Gives your marriage clear direction.

- Helps you live intentionally by clarifying what is really important to you as a couple.

- Inspires romance. Find a couple who dreams about their future together and you'll find two people madly in love.

- Reawakens passion. It's exciting and energizing to think about what can be accomplished together.

The most powerful benefit of dreaming together is the synergy it creates. The *Oxford English Dictionary* defines synergy as "the cooperation of two or more elements to produce a combined effect greater than the sum of their separate effects."[1] What you can do together is far greater than what you can do on your own. Your combined abilities, experiences, gifting, talents, and passions create an incredible God-blessed synergy—the two become one. This oneness is a superpower. When a couple is unified, they can accomplish amazing feats together. God wants us to use our superpower, our oneness, to bless others.

Hebrews 13:16 says, "Do not neglect to do good and to share what you have, for such sacrifices are pleasing to God." Sacrifice is giving away something that we *own* and *value*. This is the highest action of love. God gives us many blessings. As our hearts are abundantly full, He wants us to share His love with others—to bless them. He doesn't want us to be takers; He wants us to be sacrificial givers. Charles and Esther Mully beautifully demonstrate true sacrifice and the power of a couple using their marriage to bless others.

The movie *Mully* is the true story of Charles Mully, who as a six-year-old boy in Kenya was abandoned and left to raise himself on the streets. Against all odds, Charles thrived and, as an adult, seemed to have everything that the world sees as success. He had a beautiful wife, eight wonderful children, a great home, and a thriving business. But after street kids steal his luxury car, Charles begins wondering whether God has something more in mind for him.

Against the better judgment of his family and friends, Charles sells his business and sets out to care for orphaned children across Kenya—street kids just like him. He founded the Mully Children's Family, the largest children's rescue, rehabilitation, and development organization in Africa, and he is now revered as "father to the fatherless."

As we watched this movie, one of the messages that struck us was how Charles's wife, Esther, handled his new calling. We can only imagine the shock and disbelief she felt when her husband announced that he was going to sell everything to care for orphans. Not only did Esther have to envision what life would be like without wealth and luxury, but also within the week of notifying his family of his intentions, Charles brought three orphans home for Esther to care for. Over time, however, Charles' dream became *their* dream as a couple.

We had a similar "Mully" moment in our marriage.

A Dream Unrequited

I (Erin) was adopted as a baby into a wonderful family. As a little girl, I used to dream of the day that I could adopt a daughter. I wanted to "pay it forward"—to do for another girl what had been done for me. I'll never forget sharing this dream with Greg before we were married.

"Hey, babe," I said to Greg on our road trip from Phoenix to Colorado, the same trip where Greg cut all of the phone lines at the seedy motel in Colorado Springs. "Would you be willing to adopt someday?" And without hesitation, he enthusiastically said he would. In hindsight, I think Greg would have agreed to just about anything in order to convince me to marry him. I should have asked for more—maybe a bigger diamond ring!

But "someday" was a long time coming.

We were engaged shortly after that conversation, and once we were married, life turned busy. Greg was pursuing a doctorate in psychology. I was working the nightshift as a labor and delivery nurse. We had our first daughter, Taylor, one month before our second wedding anniversary. Then we added our second daughter, Murphy, into the mix a few years later. Shortly after Murphy was born, I returned to graduate school and completed my dream of getting a master's degree in counseling. Then came our son, Garrison. Our plates were full. Consequently, my dream of adopting was placed on the back burner.

And yet, I never lost the passion to adopt. While Greg wasn't openly resistant to the idea at this point, he wasn't thrilled about it either. He had a difficult time with the idea of adding a fourth child into our busy family. Plus, we were pursuing a new dream of doing marriage ministry together.

Several wise advisers told me that if one spouse isn't fully on board with a dream, then set it aside until unity is reached. So we did that. But I continued to pray that if we were "wrong" and were shutting the door on adoption because of our own desires or comfort, that the Lord would reveal Himself in a way that we could not deny Him. Essentially, I prayed, "Lord, drop a baby on our porch," even though our home didn't have a porch!

Several years later, we were teaching a marriage conference in Wisconsin. We encouraged the couples to spend time praying for a shared vision. So, as good teachers, we participated in this exercise as well.

I will never forget the day. The sky was slightly overcast as we walked around the picturesque lake. There were large trees billowing over the water, and the laughter of families playing together filled the air. It was a perfect Norman Rockwell moment. We sat on an old wooden bench and prayed together: "Lord, what do You want us to do *together* to bless others?" We would pray and then talk. And then pray some more. Then it happened. We both had an undeniable peace that it was time to adopt. By that beautiful lakeshore, my dream became "our" dream. We even decided to name our adopted daughter, Antoinette Rose, after my mom. That day we actively started praying for our "Annie."

Seven years passed and no Annie.

Then one day, a good friend, Kelly, was telling us about his recent trip to China. Swiping through some pictures, he paused on one showing him holding the most beautiful little Chinese girl.

"She's gorgeous," I said while grabbing his phone for a closer look.

"She's an amazing little girl," Kelly said smiling. "She's at an orphanage in Beijing. She needs hand surgery, and I'm hoping to connect the orphanage director with a doctor that I know."

Do you ever have those moments when God clearly prompts you to pray?

"Let's pray for her surgery," Greg jumped in. "Do you remember her name?"

"No," Kelly responded while trying to think. "But it was an English name."

So we started to pray for this young orphan.

"Annie," Kelly interrupted Greg's prayer. "I just remembered her name is Annie."

Greg and I were speechless. We looked at each other in disbelief. *Annie.* Could this be her? After all, we had been praying for an Annie. But we had always assumed that we would adopt a child and rename her Annie. We never thought that the name itself would be the connection.

As tears streamed down my cheeks, I smiled at Kelly. "I think you just introduced us to our daughter." It felt like our prayer had finally been answered.

As Greg and I pursued adopting Annie, God continued to confirm and guide us through circumstances, His Word, and godly counsel. I began calling adoption agencies, and I heard over and over, "You cannot handpick a child in China. Once your paperwork is complete, the government will assign you a child." But we serve a God that is bigger than government regulations!

I called every adoption agency listed online. Finally, Holt International responded. They told me to give them all of Annie's information and they would research her situation. However, they had only one stipulation: They could make no promises or guarantees. In the meantime, we started our paperwork. And by "paperwork," we mean the endless documents, questionnaires, forms, surveys, and certificates. Greg swears that Annie's paperwork took more time to finish than most of the books he's written!

We love thinking back to how faithful the Lord was as we walked forward. One day, I almost gasped when I found a picture of Annie on the orphanage's website. Her date of birth was listed across the bottom of the photo: July 23. What was significant about the date, you might be wondering? Over the years we had a running joke with our biological children that since they had all been born on the 23rd or 30th, that Annie's birthday would have to be the 23rd or the 30th. This was the first of many confirmations that the Lord provided. We also found out that Annie's nanny was a precious Chinese woman named Rose. Remember, seven years before, we had named the girl we were going to adopt, "Antoinette Rose." Again, the Lord blew us away!

The months of waiting to be matched with Annie were emotionally exhausting. Even amid God's sweet confirmations, I continued to have doubts. At times, my heart would become gripped by fear. At night, I would lie awake thinking, *How can I do this? I have three older children and Annie has special needs. There will never be enough of me to meet everyone's needs.* However, anytime I was flooded with fear Greg was like a rock. He was absolutely sure that we were fully equipped to care for Annie and our other children. And when Greg was overwhelmed with the financial aspect of this journey, I would have a peace that God would provide. It was amazing how much we were able to encourage each other throughout this difficult journey. When one of us was overwhelmed, the other was strong. And vice versa. This is the power of two! "It's better to have a partner than go it alone. . . . If one falls down, the other helps" (Ecclesiastes 4:9-10, MSG).

And then one cold January night, as we were watching a movie, I received a call on my cell phone. The voice on the other end changed our lives forever. "We got Annie's file!" our Holt social worker said enthusiastically. "Annie is officially your daughter."

Greg and I started weeping. Our tears quickly became screams of joy. The kids came running out of their beds, worried that our house was on fire! The scene in our family room looked like a game of ring-around-the-rosy. We were all holding hands, jumping around in a big circle, screaming and laughing. We finally all fell down on our knees praising God.

The dream that had formed in my eight-year-old heart, the dream that had become a shared dream with my husband and our three biological children, had finally come to fruition thirty-four years later! "But they who wait for the LORD shall renew their strength; they shall mount up with wings like eagles; they shall run and not be weary; they shall walk and not faint" (Isaiah 40:31). All that was left was to bring Annie home. However, we should have expected that once in China, we'd be greeted by Murphy's law: *Whatever can go wrong, will go wrong*!

When Dreams Don't Go as Planned

In June 2010, all five Smalleys boarded a plane to Beijing to bring our Annie home.

The anticipation was palpable. We spent the first week in China at Annie's orphanage, serving the children and the staff. It became crystal clear that Annie was not happy about us being there. She was almost three years old and had watched many of her friends get taken away by strangers. She would have nothing to do with us.

We had to travel to Annie's birth province to finalize the adoption. We were in a hotel, in Jiangxi, Nanchang, China, when there was a knock on the door. It was finally happening! We slowly opened the door and greeted Annie, who was holding a social worker's hand with one hand and a plastic bag with all her belongings in the other. "Welcome home!" the five of us shouted with glee.

Annie took one look at us, broke free of her social worker's grip, and ran off down the hallway screaming. Our son, Garrison, who was nine at the time, innocently asked, "Well . . . will they bring us another one?"

We nervously laughed, not sure what we were supposed to do. We quickly realized the social worker was waiting for us to pursue Annie. Thus began the challenges of bonding and attachment.

We found Annie hiding behind a plant down the hallway. For the next several hours, we tried to console her as she screamed. I've never experienced such heart-wrenching agony. In a healthy sense psychologically, Annie had been very attached to her nanny. She wasn't ready to let her go and open her heart to us quite yet. She was grieving the loss of her "mama." Even though we had studied this in theory, it was brutal to experience first-hand. And then something happened that we weren't prepared for.

The next day when Annie woke up, she wanted nothing to do with *me*! I (Erin) was dumbfounded. Didn't Annie understand that she was *my* dream first! Sure, adoption had become a shared dream with Greg, but it had been born in my heart. How could Annie reject me?

I understand in hindsight that it cost Annie nothing to open her heart to Greg and my other children. There had been no significant men in her life while living in her orphanage. Annie was used to having many other children around. However, she loved Rose so much that to love me would cost her everything that she held dear. I understood that in my brain. But to experience the rejection in person was so discouraging.

Annie adored every other Smalley family member, kissing their faces and giggling with them. On the other hand, I wasn't allowed near her. Annie would hit and kick me whenever I was within reach. And in spite of the rejection, I refused to believe anything other than that she was my daughter. There were days I didn't handle my emotions very well. Greg and I had the nastiest fight in the lobby of that hotel. We'll spare you the ugly details!

I continued to ask the Lord for His strength and for Annie to let me in. After three long weeks in China, I can remember boarding the plane in Beijing to fly back to the States. We were all exhausted and ready to be home. Annie still wouldn't let me near her. I looked up into the hazy sky and prayed, "Lord, I trust You. I don't get this. You brought my whole family along so they could witness a three-year-old beating me! Really? But I know this is Your will for us. Beyond a shadow of a doubt You brought Annie into our family. I will continue to trust You, knowing that her rejection may never change."

I believed in my heart that Annie and I would eventually bond, but as a counselor I understood reactive attachment disorder and I knew in my brain that some adopted children never attach. I boarded that plane that smoggy day in Beijing, giving my heart to the Lord, trusting that He had good things for our new family of six.

The rejection continued at home. We began to recognize the spiritual battle that was going on underneath the surface as well. Crazy things went on in our home, but God was faithful to give us the time and the energy to continue to pursue a new "normal" as a family. I have personally never worked on making something happen, with absolutely no ability to control the response, as I did trying to build safety in my relationship with Annie.

Greg eventually had to return to work, so it was just Annie and me. She still wasn't excited about me and more or less tolerated me feeding and changing her. She still preferred Greg and the girls. But I wasn't giving up!

I will never forget taking Annie to the doctor and having our pediatrician look at me with compassion and say, "I won't judge you if you feel like you've made a mistake." And I immediately responded, "No! This was not a mistake! This was what God had for all of us!" My fierce nature was being used to its full potential—I wasn't giving up on my Annie!

During those first weeks at home we did a lot of swimming. Not only were the Arkansas summers hot and sticky, but I was also told that swimming was a great activity to promote attachment. So, especially after our air conditioner went out mid-July, we spent as much time as we could in the water.

Every day the same routine played out. Annie would stand on the edge of the pool, ready to jump into the cool water. I would stand there with my arms outstretched, begging her to "jump to Mama! Jump to Mama." Nada. Nothing. Instead, Annie would jump to Taylor or Murphy. Each day the Lord would give me the strength to lift my arms and beseech Annie to jump to me. There were days when I lost heart, and then somehow God would give me the strength to go through the rejection again. It's almost like He knows a thing or two about rejection.

And then the day finally came!

It was late afternoon and we were swimming for a second time that day. Annie and I played our little "game" once again. She stood with her little toes on the edge of the pool. The older girls thought I was crazy trying to coerce Annie into my arms. But, once again, I gave her the opportunity. The girls looked at me and said, "Mom, just let her jump to us." And then it happened. Annie looked right at them and said, "No! I want Mama!" Annie immediately jumped into my longing arms. And from that day forward, we have been inseparable—two peas in a pod. My second miracle had finally happened!

As the Lord continued to bring peace, assurance, and joy amid waiting for our Annie, He will meet you in your journey of pursuing the desires He has placed in your heart. Let him lead and let him bring the confirmations along the way. He knows what will speak intimately to your hearts, and you *will* feel His presence.

Back to the Future

We cannot encourage you enough to return to dreaming as a couple. God united you together in oneness to do something amazing. Your marriage should be about something bigger than individual gratification, petty arguments, and the pursuit of pleasure. Inwardly focused marriages are not fulfilling. Others need to be blessed by your marriage. A shared dream will help you continue producing fruit in your marriage. Our dream was to add to our family through adoption. You may be dreaming about something different. When we have asked couples about their shared dreams, we have heard many different responses over the years:

- Raise godly children
- Get out of debt so we can financially support a ministry
- Coach a youth sports team together
- Bake cookies for a retirement home
- Provide foster care
- Serve veterans
- Adopt a child
- Go on short-term mission trips
- Volunteer at a local food bank or homeless shelter
- Work with troubled youth
- Mentor a young married couple
- Serve single parents in our church
- Help troubled marriages
- Volunteer at a women's shelter or crisis pregnancy center
- Provide respite care for parents of foster children
- Tutor immigrants studying for the citizen test

- Become a foster grandparent
- Start a new business together
- Build homes for Habitat for Humanity
- Serve on the mission field in Africa
- Start a ministry for the homeless in our city
- Become youth pastors
- Write a book together
- Minister to Olympic ice skaters

The possibilities are endless. It really doesn't matter what you pursue. The true impact is that you are united in vision and are pursuing something together that will bless others. Just like Aquila and Priscilla.

One of the earliest known missionary couples, Priscilla and Aquila, had a powerful marriage dream to spread the Gospel and serve the early church. They lived, worked, and traveled with the apostle Paul. Priscilla and Aquila worked together as tentmakers, but their shared ministry was to preach the Gospel, open their home for the meeting of the local church, and show hospitality to traveling preachers. Paul often acknowledged them by name and expressed his gratitude. As a married couple, they are credited with instructing Apollos, a major evangelist of the first century. Their names appear together six times in the New Testament, where they are described as helping to strengthen the early Christian churches. What's fascinating is that whenever they are mentioned in Scripture, they are *always* mentioned together, never separately. They were inseparable! This shows the power of a married couple actively pursuing a shared dream to serve God and to bless others.

We also wonder if another aspect of their shared dream was to demonstrate equality in marriage—husbands and wives as *joint* heirs in the faith (1 Peter 3:7). When their names are mentioned, Aquila's name is mentioned first three times and Priscilla's name is mentioned first on three occasions. This speaks to their status as equals. In a time when wives were seen as nothing more than their husband's property, Paul

RECONNECTED

makes it clear that Priscilla and Aquila are equal partners in ministry and marriage. Priscilla is thought by some to be the anonymous author of Hebrews.[2]

Like Priscilla and Aquila, we believe that every couple has a great calling on their marriage—not just individual callings. We are confident that God knows the potential you have as a couple. Much like we did while walking around the beautiful lake in Wisconsin, take some time and discuss these questions:

- What might God be calling us to do together to serve Him and bless others?
- What are some common goals, hopes, and dreams we can pursue together?
- What do we want our life together to be like five years from now? Ten years? Twenty years? Fifty years?
- At the end of our life together, what accomplishments do we want to be able to look back over and celebrate?
- What qualities do we want people to remember about us?
- What values do we want to pass on to our children and grandchildren?
- In what specific ways are we creating a marriage worth repeating for our children?
- What kind of legacy do we want to leave?

Commit to prayer whatever the Lord begins revealing to you and your spouse. You may wait for your answer for years. Or God may answer you much faster than you expect. Matthew 7:7 from *The Message* says, "Be direct. Ask [God] for what you need." And then trust in God's timing. He knows what is best for your marriage and those who will be impacted by your dream.

We know some of you are thinking, *Oh, sure—easy for you to say that the Lord will meet our needs. It all worked out for you, but we aren't Greg*

194

and Erin Smalley. The truth is we had no idea how this whole adoption dream would play out. However, we were always confident in the Lord's faithfulness. He confirmed that Annie was our child through her name, her nanny's name, Annie's date of birth, and even how He revealed her to us. He cares about the desires of your heart—He put them there. However, give the reins over to Him and let Him lead. He knows the outcome.

We are convinced that dreaming is less about the final outcome and much more about the journey you are on with your spouse and the Lord. Pursuing a shared dream breeds such a deep level of intimacy and connection in your relationship both with God and with your spouse.

Don't ever stop dreaming together. When one dream comes to fruition or unexpectedly ends, start praying about what the Lord has next for you as a couple. Once Annie was home and we were settled in, we began praying and asking God, "What's next, Lord?" We believed that the Lord was calling us to marriage ministry together, which didn't even make sense because, upon bringing Annie home, we had committed to no traveling for one year. However, within the next few months, Greg ran into Jim Daly, the president and CEO of Focus on the Family, in the Dallas/Fort Worth airport. Greg came home saying, "Jim wants to talk about an opportunity." Greg met Jim the next morning for breakfast, and sure enough, he shared with Greg the vision of bringing on a couple to head up their newly formed marriage division. As we prayed and sought wisdom, we ended up making the move to Colorado Springs and beginning our journey with Focus on the Family. We love helping couples learn how to have a marriage they are both thrilled with. And when we're working side-by-side, we experience a type of intimacy and connection that is difficult to put into words. Honestly, the communication is awesome between us, and the sex is never better! I'm just being honest.

When you're living out your shared dreams, we truly believe that God blesses your relationship in amazing ways. There is something beautiful about two souls imagining a future together and then working every day to accomplish this shared vision. This is the essence of "two becoming one" in marriage!

As you dream in your marriage, continue to allow the Lord to lead you. It's like the song, "Nothing I Hold On To" by Will Reagan and United Pursuit. There is a powerful line in the song that says, "I give it all to You, God, trusting that You'll make something beautiful out of me." Trust that the Lord is making something beautiful out of your marriage. Remember, that this is much more about the journey together than the end result. He will use the challenges, turns in the road, and mountaintop experiences to mold you and your marriage into His image. Amid the challenges, look for Him and know that He intimately will speak to your heart in a way that no one else can. He will meet your needs as you both continue to cry out to Him. The benefits of dreaming together are too great to allow your marriage to be dreamless! Therefore, go "back to the future" and dream together!

Roommates have no long-term plans;

soulmates pursue shared dreams together.

CHAPTER 13

The Story of Us

Marriage is a mosaic you build with your spouse.

Millions of tiny moments that create your love story.

JENNIFER SMITH

Roommates are a temporary arrangement;

soulmates persevere through the hard times and

recognize the power of their love story.

WE LOVE A GOOD LOVE STORY. But more importantly, we believe telling our love story is one of the most powerful ways we can keep our marriage strong. The good news is it's not the particulars of our story that matter—it's "how" we tell it that's most important. According to marriage researcher Dr. John Gottman, he can predict with 94 percent accuracy if a couple will make it based solely on how they tell their story.[1] That's astounding. In Gottman's study, couples who had a positive view of their history together were more likely to stay together. Happy couples talked about their relationship in a positive way and filtered the early days through a rose-colored lens—a relationship filled with good times. They were able to see their challenges as both painful and as experiences that grew them as a couple. Unhappy couples, however, focused more on the difficult times—the pain and the struggles. Sadly, they edited out the good times as anomalies and altered their history to reflect their current state of unhappiness.

We are constantly telling our stories. I (Greg) have a list of more than 550 stories about our marriage and family. We use these for the marriage seminars we teach, but we also tell them to our children and friends as well. Author Jerry Jenkins has a wonderful perspective about sharing your story:

> Tell your [marriage] story. Tell it to your kids, your friends, your brothers and sisters, but especially to each other. The more your story is implanted in your brain, the more it serves as a hedge against the myriad of forces that seek to destroy your marriage. Make your story so familiar that it becomes part of the fabric of your being. It should become a legend that is shared through the generations as you grow a family tree that defies all odds and boasts marriage after marriage of stability, strength, and longevity.[2]

We want our love story to inspire our children. We want to create a marriage worth repeating! After all, our marriage is their blueprint for their future relationships. They need to hear us talk about the fun times, the good times, the hard times—all of it—but from a positive viewpoint. We want to remind them that God has brought us far.

Greg and Erin Smalley—est. May 30, 1992

In ancient Rome, it was considered bad luck to get out of bed on the left side. Therefore, if you got out of bed on the "wrong" side (the left side), it was assumed that you would have a very bad day.[3]

In our second year of marriage, we experienced this type of Roman bad day! We both woke up feeling grumpy, and everything we did or said seemed to annoy the other. It was like we'd both woken up on the wrong side of bed.

At some point that morning, we were arguing about something

trivial when Erin intervened, "We need to stop talking! I'm not sure why we're fighting. If there really is an issue, let's discuss it tonight after we've had time to cool off and get perspective."

I (Greg) stood there dumbfounded, my mouth wide open. Erin had previously said something that I badly wanted to refute, but now she had set a pretty healthy boundary, so I stopped talking mid-sentence. "Fine," I responded, rolling my eyes.

We spent the rest of the morning in peaceful silence.

When Erin was finished getting ready, she headed for the front door of our tiny fourth floor apartment.

We kissed each other goodbye (it was more like two pecking chickens than passionate lovers) and then Erin left.

Suddenly, the front door swung open, Erin popped her head back into our apartment, where she made one final point pertaining to our earlier conversation, and then quickly shut the door.

Again, I was dumbfounded. What had just happened? Erin had violated the "no talking" boundary that she'd set earlier. I had respected her request even though I had plenty more that I wanted to "share." Worse yet, she had just gotten in the last word. What sort of precedence would this establish in our young marriage?

I wanted to chase her down the hallway and right the injustice that had just taken place. I opened the front door but discovered that Erin was already gone.

"That's just great!" I muttered under my breath.

After a few minutes of sulking, I started to gather my things to leave the apartment. As I was walking out, I suddenly remembered that I was supposed to take our dirty clothes down to the laundry room and start the washer.

Let me pause and explain one important detail. At the time, Erin and I did the laundry very differently. She used her great grandmother's tiny antique basket. But the basket was so small that she had to make multiple trips up and down the four flights of stairs. It seemed exhausting!

I, on the other hand, like to do things the easy way. Instead of using the miniature fourth-generation antique basket, I purchased a gigantic mesh bag from Dollar General. Since the laundry room was directly under our apartment on the first floor, I would stuff all of the dirty clothes in the huge bag, drag it out to the railing, and drop it bombardier style. I allowed gravity to do all of the work. It was a brilliant plan unless you've recently experienced a fight with your wife where she got in the last word!

After heaving the mammoth bag on top of the balcony railing, I was just about to release it, when I noticed Erin walking toward me on the ground floor. I was confused. She had left fifteen minutes before. She probably stopped to visit with a friend. Extroverts!

Regardless, there she was, and I was still struggling with the enormous mesh bag balancing precariously on the tiny railing. But that was also the exact moment that a spectacularly unwise plan began to form in my fevered brain.

I decided to show my unsuspecting bride how to really get "the last word."

So, as Erin casually passed under our apartment, I released my grip on the bag.

Before we discuss my aim, I swear on a stack of Bibles, that I never actually wanted to hit my wife. I just wanted to startle her. I was simply trying to make my "last word" point by dropping our clothes *near* her. Then I'd pretend, "Oh, I'm sorry. I was just dropping the laundry." I know, vintage passive-aggressive behavior!

Unfortunately, my dumb-bomb clipped her. It didn't crush her neck or anything nearly so disastrous, but it did launch her off her feet and knock her to the floor. As she lay sprawled out on the walkway, she looked up—and saw me still looking over the railing in disbelief.

At that instant it dawned on me: *I'm in big trouble.*

While I knew Erin had run track in college, I never fully realized how fast she could climb stairs. I had only seconds to decide what to do. Erin is tough, and I didn't know whether she would pummel me or sling me over the railing to join my laundry bag.

So I did what any man would do if faced with a similar dilemma. I hastily retreated into our apartment and quickly turned the lock. Seconds later I heard Erin banging furiously on the door. I slinked back against the wall, careful not to make a sound, madly hoping that she might think I had run off. I knew one thing: Whatever happened, I was *not* about to open that door!

Our worried neighbors heard the commotion and started streaming out of their apartments, and their curiosity saved me—literally saved me. Unnerved by all the watching eyes, Erin bounded down the stairs and drove off in a cloud of dust.

By the time I (Erin) returned home that night, Greg had washed and folded every stitch of clothing in our apartment to make amends. The dozen piles of laundry were strategically positioned around the living room. Greg had even washed our couch cushion covers. Unfortunately, he also dried them. So, when I returned that night, the shrunken covers made our couch cushions look like misshapen pyramids.

Somehow we smoothed things over that evening. The new couch probably helped.

This story, "the laundry debacle" as we affectionately call it, represents one of many crazy stories that have happened over our twenty-seven years of marriage.

I (Greg) love this story because it so perfectly characterizes the early years of our marriage: unbelievable, passionate, funny, wild, conflicted, idiotic, depressing, and miraculous.

At a recent marriage event, we were telling this story and a woman approached me at a break. "That's a terrible story," she explained with a half-smile. "I can't believe Erin stayed married to you."

But that's what makes this story so amazing—she *did* stay with me. Erin still loves me, and I'm madly in love with her. The laundry debacle represents the good, the bad, and the ugly of our early marriage. And we're able to laugh about it now.

I wouldn't trade this story, or any of the 550 that I keep on my computer, because collectively, they define our relationship: We've experienced amazing times and we've been through difficult seasons in our marriage, but by God's grace and mercy, we are more than conquerors (Romans 8:37).

We understand how God used those early years to shape us as individuals and as a couple into the marriage we now have. We love our marriage, but it wouldn't be the same relationship today if we hadn't gone through those difficulties and learned from them. Although I'm still not allowed to use a mesh laundry bag!

Retelling Your Story

Think back to Dr. John Gottman's ability to predict with 94 percent accuracy couples that will and won't make it based solely on how they tell their story. That's incredible. The happy couples talk about their relationship in a positive way. They have a positive view of their history together. They see a relationship filled with good times and redemption. Unhappy couples, however, focus more on the difficult times—the disappointments, the struggles, and the pain.

The good news is it's not the particulars of your story that matter—it's how you tell it. The narrative, the words you use, and the details you share are what's important.

I (Erin) saw a couple for counseling, and I'll never forget how Stacy portrayed their story during our first session.

"We met on a blind date in college," Stacy began. "I wasn't really attracted to Brian at first. It definitely wasn't 'love at first sight.' He was more on the husky side, and he was an introvert. I was typically drawn to good-looking, outgoing men.

"We sporadically dated over the next few months. However, one night,

I was feeling really lonely. My roommates were all happily dating, and I was jealous. After sulking for a few hours, I called Brian. I didn't want to be alone, and he was the only guy I knew who wasn't a complete jerk.

"Well, we took things too far that night and I ended up pregnant. I was so stupid! I wasn't really attracted to him. How could this happen after having sex only once—and it wasn't even that great! But there I was: young, single, and pregnant. Obviously, I had to drop out of college after I decided to keep my baby.

"Brian is a decent guy, and he was around during my pregnancy. We continued to see each other over the next nine months. But it wasn't like we were dating. So, you can imagine how shocked I was when Brian proposed in the hospital room. He knew how religious my parents were and how they felt about us having a child outside of marriage. Brian actually got the hospital chaplain to marry us before I went into labor. Not exactly the fairy-tale wedding I'd dreamed about my entire life!

"Our marriage is so different than I ever imagined. I thought I'd marry someone I was madly in love with and that we'd have this passionate relationship. Brian is more like a dependable friend—a roommate. I respect him for marrying me, and we share our children in common. But the love and passion have always been missing. I'm not sure that I've ever loved Brian. I said yes to his proposal because I felt guilty, and I wanted our child to grow up with his father. Sadly, that probably wasn't the best reason to get married.

"Another part of the problem is that I've always resented Brian because I had to drop out of college. I had big dreams. I wanted to be a teacher and work overseas. I had to give up my dreams once I got pregnant."

After a long tearful pause, Stacy ended her story by saying, "I'm just not sure that our marriage can be salvaged."

The entire time that Stacy unpacked her version of their love story, Brian sat there in complete silence. It was heart-wrenching to listen to

Stacy's perception of their eight-year marriage. They both seemed so hopeless.

According to Dr. Gottman's research, Brian and Stacy should be a divorce statistic. But we serve a mighty God—a God who is passionate about marriage. Brian and Stacy had the God of this universe in their corner fighting for their marriage. And God is in the restoration business. I will never forget when Stacy said, "I'm just not sure that our marriage can be salvaged." I loved her choice of words. In our culture, salvage is often equated with junk or garbage. The phrase "junk yard" is often synonymous with "salvage yard." But salvage doesn't mean junk. Salvage is something extracted (as from garbage) as valuable or useful.[4] When you salvage a ship, you are saving something valuable (i.e., its cargo) from the perils of the seas. When a marriage is salvaged, God is saving something of high value from ruin. Even when a marriage looks like it's in complete ruin, there is always hope that God will salvage this treasured relationship.

I (Erin) spent months counseling this hurting couple. And it wasn't easy. Their journey was a roller coaster full of ups and downs, twists and turns. There were times that I thought we'd gotten over the hump only to find them discouraged the next week. Their progress felt like two tiny steps forward, one giant step back. I would constantly remind them that the struggle was only *part* of their story, but it wasn't their *whole* story. The ending had yet to be written.

Strength never comes from winning. When you go through adversity and don't give up, that's true strength. This is exactly what I watched happen to Brian and Stacy.

Years after we ended our counseling relationship, Brian and Stacy joined the marriage ministry team at their church. After recommending Greg and me as speakers for their annual marriage conference, we got to hear them share their testimony from the stage. I was blown away!

Brain and Stacy held hands as they shared their marriage story—a very different version from the one I'd heard five years earlier.

"Brian and I met on a blind date. I'll never forget his kind looking eyes. I was instantly drawn to his gentle nature. We dated sporadically and ended up getting pregnant. I was so scared. I was used to being abandoned by the men in my life. But Brian was different. He instantly stepped up and supported me throughout my pregnancy. He was a great friend.

Looking at Brian she said, "I'm sure I treated you poorly. I was resentful that I had to drop out of school . . ."

Brian interrupted his wife, "I knew that wasn't who you were." Brian put his arm around Stacy. "You were scared and hurting. Besides, you weren't getting rid of me that easy."

The crowd chuckled.

"I loved Stacy with all my heart," Brian continued as his wife's eyes welled up with tears. "I wanted her to be my wife. But I wanted her to know that it wasn't just because we were having a child together. A few weeks before Stacy's due date, I asked her father for permission to marry her. After getting her father's blessing, I asked the hospital chaplain if he'd marry us in the delivery room. I know it was a strange request, but I really wanted to surprise Stacy. I asked Stacy's mom if she could decorate our hospital room with Stacy's favorite flowers. She loved . . ."

"Wait," Stacy interrupted. "The calla lilies were your idea?"

"Yes." Brian smiled.

Tears once again subdued the normally talkative Stacy.

"Stacy loved calla lilies," Brian explained. "So I had her mother fill our hospital room with dozens of them. The chaplain pronounced us 'husband and wife' minutes before you went into labor, remember?"

"I do," Stacy gently responded with a cracked voice. "Although it wasn't the wedding that I'd dreamed about, I wouldn't change a thing. I love that unique detail of our story. Most people get married in a church. I got married on a fully adjustable hospital bed with a built-in panic button."

"I should have pushed the panic button," Brian joked, ribbing his wife.

The crowd roared with laughter.

"To be honest," Stacy explained, "our marriage journey hasn't been easy. Please don't misunderstand me. There have been great moments, like the birth of our two children, the Hawaiian honeymoon that we finally got to take, Brian supporting me as I completed my teaching degree, family vacations, date nights, and our involvement here at church. But there have been some really dark times as well. About eight years into our marriage, I finally reached a breaking point. I didn't want to be married anymore. My fantasies about love and marriage were so different than reality. My heart hardened, and I was done. But Brian's love never wavered. Although I couldn't see it at the time, his gentle nature was like a mighty rock. Those kind eyes never hardened . . ."

Stacy trailed off as tears streamed down her cheeks.

"It wasn't me," Brian countered. "It was God. Those were some tough years. When Stacy's heart hardened, I felt so helpless and alone. There were plenty of times that I felt so discouraged that I wanted to give up. But I knew God was bigger than our issues. I did a whole lot of praying during those dark times. And God was faithful. God brought us Erin Smalley. We spent months in counseling, and God used Erin to help restore our marriage."

Stacy chimed in, "Erin, you were a godsend. You are an amazing counselor. Although it took me some time to realize, I loved this man . . . this hot-stud of a man."

Brian beamed as his wife flirted with him.

"And why we're so honored to introduce our special guest speakers, Erin and her husband, Greg."

That's how you tell a love story!

We've been speaking together for fifteen years and that's still my most favorite introduction. It's not because I got top billing over my husband (although that was nice). It was watching a couple who seemed so hopeless when I met them be transformed through Christ. Before hearing their marriage testimony, I used to say to other therapy couples, "At least your story isn't like this one couple who I worked with years ago . . . that was brutal." Seriously, Stacy's rendition of their marriage story was so negative that I was certain that they'd be nothing more than one of Gottman's statistics—one of the ones who didn't make it.

Brian and Stacy's testimony is exactly what Dr. Gottman discovered through his research. When couples have a positive view of their marital history, they are more likely to stay together. Happy couples brag about the good times. But more than talking about the good times, happy couples boast about hard times. They routinely discuss how painful challenges grew them as individuals and as a couple.

When telling their story, happy couples hit the "high points," the "low points," and the "turning points." They talk about their highs. But they also talk honestly about their lows—the pain and suffering. They disclose the irritations, nasty conflicts, heartaches, loss, broken trust, parenting challenges, bankruptcy, job loss, prodigal children, in-law battles, lost friendships, spiritual disappointments, and so on. However, they always end with the turning points—the lessons learned, the personal growth, the benefits gained, counseling insights, moments of redemption, and being part of God's larger narrative.

Author Dave Willis explains, "Your story is important, but more importantly it should be wrapped up in the Story bigger than you."[5] We couldn't agree more. Your marriage is much more than just a collection of dates, facts, and anecdotes. There is a bigger purpose behind your marriage story. Your marriage is part of God's storyline. The larger narrative for your marriage is that your love for each other should be the evidence that you are a follower of Christ. This is exactly what Brian and Stacy modeled—that Christ makes a difference in a marriage.

Another important part of telling your story is acknowledging God's help and constant presence. Happy couples boast about the truth of Romans 8:28: "And we know that for those who love God all things work together for good, for those who are called according to his purpose." Even when God seems far away, He is always with us, protecting us and growing us. Happy couples recognize that we *all* have clear examples of God doing amazing things in our marriages and families. Your marriage has a sworn enemy. Satan hates your marriage because he knows what a united couple is capable of doing for the kingdom. Satan fears your marriage. This is why he continues his endless assault on your relationship.

When you turn toward God and ask Him for help in your marriage, you must expect Satan to muster all his forces in battle against you. But there is always hope in God. One of our most precious examples of this was when our mentors, Gary and Carrie Oliver, walked into our marriage.

We had only been married a few years. We were really struggling relationally. This was probably right about the time of the laundry debacle. But we won't get into that again!

One day, Erin was out perusing the shops at our local mall. I (Greg) was home in our apartment when our home phone rang. As I picked up the receiver (this was long before cell phones), I heard Carrie Oliver's cheerful voice on the other end. "Hello, Greg," Carrie greeted me, "May I speak to your lovely wife?"

"Sorry," I explained, "she's not here."

"When do you expect her back?" Carrie asked.

"I really have no idea," I answered.

"Oh," Carrie's voice now seemed concerned. "Is everything okay?"

In these moments, my proclivity toward humor and banter can get me into big trouble.

"Erin's gone," I joked. "She left me."

I stood there holding the phone, smiling at my wittiness, thinking, *I crack myself up.*

However, apparently Carrie didn't realize that I was joking. And after several seconds of long, awkward silence, Carrie finally responded, "Greg, I'm so sorry. Gary and I have been worried that this might happen."

"Ha ha," I sarcastically bantered back. "You guys were right. Thankfully there are plenty of fish in the sea."

"That's horrible!" Carrie scolded. "Why would you say that?"

"What?" I quickly responded. Suddenly I felt very confused and uncertain if we *both* were exchanging banter. "You know I'm joking, right?"

Again, after a long pause, Carrie spoke, "I actually thought you were serious. If I'm being honest, Gary and I have been worried about you guys for some time. I think we need to have a serious talk. Can you and Erin come over tonight?"

We promise we're not making this up. Greg and Carrie actually had this conversation on the phone. But thank God. In reality, we weren't okay. Sure, I (Erin) might not have left Greg for someone I met at the mall that day, but we were really struggling in our marriage. We believe that God prompted Carrie in the midst of Greg's "not so funny" banter. We did go over to the Oliver's house that night. And it was powerful. For the first time, we were honest about our marriage problems. We cried a lot telling our story. But we also left with hope. Over the next several years, Gary and Carrie poured into our marriage and interceded on our behalf. Our marriage is what it is today because of their investment and God's faithfulness. Happy couples give credit to God as the Author of our love story.

Stories like the laundry debacle remind us that we've come a long way and that we're pretty good together. Through the laughter, we're reminded of why we got married in the first place. But most importantly, reminiscing helps us to anticipate an enjoyable future together.

Awaken, O Sleeper!

The main antagonist in C. S. Lewis's book *The Lion, the Witch and the Wardrobe* is a powerful sorceress called the White Witch. The unfortunate souls who displease or challenge her are not just imprisoned, but frozen: turned into statues made of stone.[6]

Satan uses this same plotline in our marriages. He hates the beautiful husband and wife union that God has created. Satan understands the power of a fully alive marriage. Satan knows what you and your spouse are capable of together, and he fears your marriage! This is why he tries to destroy marriage one little fox at a time. We've tried to make the point throughout this book that it's usually not the big issues (e.g., infidelity, pornography, abuse, addictions) that destroy a marriage. Most marriages die from a slow fade—when couples slowly drift apart over the years. I (Greg) was just reading about a celebrity couple who was getting a divorce. The reason cited was, "I guess we grew out of love."[7]

Don't let the little foxes destroy the delicious fruit in your marriage. You don't have to "grow out of love." God wants us to not only enjoy this mysterious relationship between a husband and a wife where we can reach the absolute deepest levels of intimacy and connection, but He also wants our marriages to reflect Him—His love, passion, humor, intimacy, grace, connection, pleasure, humility, and forgiveness. He wants our marriages to act as a lighthouse in a dark world. Our marriages should be the greatest evangelistic tool that demonstrates that Christ makes a difference in our lives and relationships.

During that first wedding ceremony between Adam and Eve, God charged them to "be fruitful and multiply" (Genesis 1:28). Fruitfulness involves more than populating the earth. A fully alive marriage blesses you. You benefit from what God created to take you to the deepest levels of intimacy and connection. However, your fully alive marriage isn't just for you. There's much more at stake than your enjoyment. It's a living testimony of God's love to a fallen world. It's a model for your children. It's evidence to a fearful generation that a thriving marriage is possible. People should be blessed by your marriage. Our children should want to get married based on what they witness in our marriage. Roommate marriages will never be fruitful or multiply what God has entrusted to us.

Like the White Witch, Satan wants to imprison us in a busy, exhausted, sexless, boring, business-like, neglected, disconnected marriage where passion becomes frozen and hearts turn to stone. We must fight back!

Like the animals of Narnia, we must wake up and realize that the slow fade is real. In the beginning of chapter sixteen of *The Lion, the Witch and the Wardrobe*, three of the main characters—Aslan, Susan, and Lucy—are in the courtyard of the Witch's palace when something amazing happens to the frozen statues and hardened hearts. Aslan literally breathes life back into Narnia, reversing the Witch's spell and setting the creatures free from the Witch's curse. One by one the statues begin to awaken, and life is restored.

Like Aslan in the "Chronicles of Narnia," Christ can breathe life back into your frozen marriage. If you're living in a roommate marriage decide that you want back what God originally designed your marriage to be.

Moving from roommates to soulmates requires you to proactively engage in soulmate behaviors as we've discussed throughout the pages of this book.

Moving from roommates to soulmates also requires time. Roommates feel like two ships passing in the night. Staying with this analogy, it requires a large ship as much as five nautical miles to stop and over a third of a mile to turn around and reverse course.[8] There are definitely some quick fixes that will make a difference, but you need to be in it for the long haul. Once a big ship commits to a turn, it will not waver. In the same way, you'll need persistent effort and investment to proactively reconnect as a couple and move toward being soulmates.

Maybe you haven't reached a crisis point in your marriage, but you feel the disconnection from living like roommates. Wherever you find yourself today, you can rediscover your soulmate and revive your sleeping marriage!

Roommates are a temporary arrangement;

soulmates persevere through the hard times and

recognize the power of their love story.

NOTES

CHAPTER 1: IN LOVE WITH A STRANGER

1. Nell Frizzell, "Why Do Relationships End? You Asked Google—Here's the Answer," *The Guardian*, August 9, 2017, https://www.theguardian.com/commentisfree/2017/aug/09/why-relationships-end-ask-google.
2. Nell Frizzell, "Why Do Relationships End? You Asked Google—Here's the Answer," *The Guardian*, August 9, 2017, https://www.theguardian.com/commentisfree/2017/aug/09/why-relationships-end-ask-google.
3. Marriage and Divorce, *American Psychological Association*, http://www.apa.org/topics/divorce/.
4. Paul R. Amato and Denise Previti, "People's Reasons for Divorcing," *Journal of Family Issues*, 24, (2003), 602–626.
5. Xenia P. Montenegro, *The Divorce Experience: A Study of Divorce at Midlife and Beyond*, (2004). Conducted for *AARP The Magazine*; http://assets.aarp.org/rgcenter/general/divorce.pdf.
6. Paul M. de Graaf and Matthijs Kalmijn, "Divorce Motives in a Period of Rising Divorce," *Journal of Family Issues*. Vol 27, Issue 4, (2006), 483–505.
7. Alan Hawkins, Brian J. Willoughby, and William J. Doherty, "Reasons for Divorce and Openness to Marital Reconciliation., *Journal of Divorce and Remarriage*, 53, (2012): 453–463; See also W.J. Doherty, S. M. Harris, and K. Wickel Didericksen, A typology of attitudes toward proceeding with divorce among parents in the divorce process. *Journal of Divorce & Remarriage*, 57, (2016):1–11.
8. "30 Odd Sexless Marriage Statistics," http://healthresearchfunding.org/sexless-marriage-statistics/.
9. Carmen Harra, "The 10 Elements of a Soulmate," *Huffington Post*, (December 23, 2013), http://www.huffingtonpost.com/dr-carmen-harra/elements-of-a-soulmate_b_3595992.html.

CHAPTER 2: FULLY ALIVE

1. "Satan's Agenda," Geraldine Harris and Kristen Maddox. © Copyright 1998-2008. All Rights Reserved. Used by permission.

2. "What's the Point of Using a Metronome?" *Musical U* (July 20, 2014), https://www.musical-u.com/learn/whats-the-point-of-using-a-metronome/.

3. John Ortberg, *The Life You've Always Wanted* (Grand Rapids, MI: Zondervan, 2015).

4. http://www.encyclopedia.com/topic/rest.aspx

5. Matthew J. Edlund, "Why We Don't 'Get' Rest," *Psychology Today*, October 6, 2011, https://www.psychologytoday.com/blog/the-power-rest/201110/why-we-dont-get-rest.

6. "Sleep Needs," *HelpGuide*, http://www.helpguide.org/articles/sleep/how-much-sleep-do-you-need.htm.

7. Yasmin Anwar, "Poor Sleep Can Leave Romantic Partners Feeling Unappreciated," *Berkeley News*, January 19, 2013, http://news.berkeley.edu/2013/01/19/sleep-couples/.

8. "Laughter Is the Best Medicine," *HelpGuide*, https://www.helpguide.org/articles/mental-health/laughter-is-the-best-medicine.htm.

9. Kalah Siegel, "The Ten Best Foods to Help Fight Stress," *Everyday Health*, March 26, 2019, https://www.everydayhealth.com/diet-nutrition-pictures/how-to-reduce-stress-with-diet.aspx.

CHAPTER 3: FROM BUSYNESS TO CONNECTION

1. John Gottman, *Why Marriages Succeed or Fail*, (Simon & Schuster, 1995), 104.

2. Zach Brittle, "Turn Towards Instead of Away," *The Gottman Institute*, April 1, 2015, https://www.gottman.com/blog/turn-toward-instead-of-away/.

3. John Gottman and Nan Silver, *The Seven Principles for Making Marriage Work*, (Harmony, 2015), 88.

4. Kyle Benson, "3 Steps to Reconnect When You Feel Disconnected from Your Partner," *The Gottman Institute*, August 26, 2016, https://www.gottman.com/blog/3-steps-reconnect-feel-disconnected-partner/.

5. Ellie Lisitsa, "An Introduction to Emotional Bids and Trust," *The Gottman Institute*, August 31, 2012, https://www.gottman.com/blog/an-introduction-to-emotional-bids-and-trust/.

6. Jenna Jonaitis, "5 Long-Time Married Couples Share Their Secrets to a Happy Marriage," *Verily*, July 7, 2017, https://verilymag.com/2017/07/secret-to-a-happy-marriage-long-time-married-couples.

CHAPTER 4: LIFE-GIVING COMMUNICATION

1. Amy Bellows, "Good Communication in Marriage Starts with Respect," *PsychCentral*, October 8, 2018, https://psychcentral.com/lib/good-communication-in-marriage-starts-with-respect/.

2. Gabrielle Frank, "What American Marriages Are Really Like in 2017," *Today*, June 26, 2017, http://www.today.com/health/what-it-s-be-married-2017-t112961.

3. Brandon Specktor, "The Most Complicated Word in English Is Only Three Letters Long," *Reader's Digest*, https://www.rd.com/culture/most-complicated-word-in-english/.

4. The saying is adapted from a line in "To a Mouse" by Robert Burns.

5. "Why Silence Is Golden After a Happy Marriage: Couples Only Speak for 3 Minutes at Dinner," *DailyMail*, April 9, 2019, http://www.dailymail.co.uk

/femail/article-1264868/Why-silence-golden-happy-marriage-Couples-speak
-3-minutes-dinner.html.

6. Sari Harrar and Rita DeMaria, *7 Stages of Marriage: Laughter, Intimacy and Passion Today, Tomorrow, Forever* (Pleasantville, NY: The Reader's Digest Association, 2006) 8.

7. Matthias R. Mehl, Simine Vazire, Shannon E. Holleran, and C. Shelby Clark, "Eavesdropping on Happiness: Well-Being Is Related to Having Less Small Talk and More Substantive Conversations," *Psychological Science*. Vol 21, Issue 4, February 18, 2010, 539–541, https://doi.org/10.1177/0956797610362675.

8. Marcia Naomi Berger, *Marriage Meetings for Lasting Love: 30 Minutes a Week to the Relationship You've Always Wanted* (New World Library, 2014) https://www.amazon
.com/Reclaiming-Conversation-Power-Talk-Digital/dp/1608682234?ie=UTF8
&camp=1789&creative=390957&creativeASIN=1608682234&linkCode=as2
&linkId=FSXA3GZUT5SFDAZ4&redirect=true&ref_=as_li_tl&tag=stucosuccess.

9. Nan Schoenberg, "Can We Talk?" *Chicago Tribune*, January 14, 2011, http://
articles.chicagotribune.com/2011-01-14/features/sc-fam-0111-talk-relationship
-20110111_1_happy-marriages-couples-marital-therapy.

10. An ongoing long-term study funded by the National Institutes of Health. Since 1986, Dr. Terri Orbuch followed the same 373 couples, who were married that year.

11. Terri Orbuch, "4 Ways the Happiest Couples Stay Happy," *Psychology Today*, February 13, 2010, https://www.psychologytoday.com/blog/the-love-doctor
/201002/4-ways-the-happiest-couples-stay-happy.

CHAPTER 5: GENTLE NEGLECT

1. Amy Novotney, "Is 'Technoference' Hurting Your Partner?" *American Psychological Association*, Vol. 47, No. 2, February 2016, https://apa.org/monitor/2016/02
/smartphone-sidebar.aspx.

2. Brandon T. McDaniel and Sarah Coyne, "Technoference: The Interference of Technology in Couple Relationships and Implications for Women's Personal and Relational Well-Being," *Psychology of Popular Media Culture*, 2014, http://psycnet
.apa.org/doi/10.1037/ppm0000065.

3. "Neglect," Vocabulary.com, https://www.vocabulary.com/dictionary/neglect.

4. James A. Roberts and Meredith E. David, "My life has become a major distraction from my cell phone: Partner phubbing and relationship satisfaction among romantic partners," *Computers in Human Behavior*, Volume 54, January 2016, 134–141.

5. "Too Much Texting Can Disconnect Couples, Research Finds," *BYU News*, October 29, 2013, https://news.byu.edu/news/too-much-texting-can-disconnect
-couples-research-finds.

6. "Siren," Wikipedia, https://en.wikipedia.org/wiki/Siren_(mythology).

7. "Sirens," GreekMythology.com, https://www.greekmythology.com/Myths/Creatures
/Sirens/sirens.html

8. "Sacred," Dictionary.com, http://www.dictionary.com/browse/sacred.

9. "Does Kissing Your Spouse Extend Your Lifespan?" *SiOWfa15: Science in Our World: Certainty and Controversy*, https://sites.psu.edu/siowfa15/2015/12/04
/does-kissing-your-spouse-extend-your-lifespan/.

10. Joshua Foer, "The Kiss of a Lifetime," *The New York Times*, February 14, 2016, http://www.nytimes.com/2006/02/14/opinion/the-kiss-of-life.html.
11. Eliza Murphy, "Anniversary Surprise for Husband at Airport: Wife Wearing Wedding Dress," *ABC News*, October 5, 2012, https://abcnews.go.com/blogs /headlines/2012/10/anniversary-surprise-for-husband-at-airport-wife-wearing -wedding-dress/.

CHAPTER 6: LIVING SEPARATE LIVES
1. Lars Tornstam, "Loneliness in marriage," *Journal of Relationships*, 9, no. 2 (May, 1992): 197–217.
2. C.M. Perissinotto, I. Stijacic Cenzer I, and K. E. Covinsky, "Loneliness in Older Persons a Predictor of Functional Decline and Death," *Arch Intern Med.* 2012;172 (14):1078–1084. doi:10.1001/archinternmed.2012.1993.
3. Darlene Lancer, "Are You Lonely in Your Marriage?" *Psychology Today*, October 29, 2017, https://www.psychologytoday.com/us/blog/toxic-relationships/201710 /are-you-lonely-in-your-marriage.
4. Dennis Rainey and Barbara Rainey, "Are You Married and Lonely?" Adapted from *Starting Your Marriage Right*, Thomas Nelson Publishers, 2000, posted on *Family Life*, http://www.familylife.com/articles/topics/marriage/staying-married /commitment/married-and-lonely.
5. "Monkey Trap," *Wiktionary*, https://en.wiktionary.org/wiki/monkey_trap.
6. Chris Weller, "How Stress Divides the Sexes: Why Do Men Withdraw While Women Become More Social?" *Medical Daily*, March 18, 2014, https://www .medicaldaily.com/how-stress-divides-sexes-why-do-men-withdraw-while-women -become-more-social-271488.
7. Sarah Treleaven, "The Science Behind Happy Relationships," *Time*, June 26, 2018, http://time.com/5321262/science-behind-happy-healthy-relationships/.
8. Sue Johnson, *Hold Me Tight: Seven Conversations for a Lifetime of Love* (Little, Brown Spark, 2008) 49–50.
9. "Baros," Bible Hub, https://biblehub.com/greek/922.htm.
10. Sue Johnson, *Hold Me Tight: Seven Conversations for a Lifetime of Love* (Little, Brown Spark, 2008) 50.
11. Lizette Borreli, "Why Couples Engage in Pillow Talk after Sex: Orgasms Increase Oxytocin Levels, Leading to Feelings of Trust," *Medical Daily*, December 27, 2013, https://www.medicaldaily.com/why-couples-engage-pillow-talk-after-sex -orgasms-increase-oxytocin-levels-leading-feelings-trust.

CHAPTER 7: REKINDLING ROMANCE AND PASSION
1. Tara Parker-Pope, "Reinventing Date Nights for Long-Married Couples," *The New York Times*, February 12, 2018, https://www.nytimes.com/2008/02/12 /health/12well.html.
2. M. F. Lorber, A. C. Erlanger, R. E. Heyman, and K. D. O'Leary, "The Honeymoon Effect: Does It Exist and Can It Be Predicted?" *The National Center for Biotechnology*, May 2015, https://www.ncbi.nlm.nih.gov/pubmed/24643282?report=abstract.

3. "Two Years, Six Months and 25 Days: The Length of Time It Takes Before Romance Is Dead," *Daily Mail*, October 29, 2008, http://www.dailymail.co.uk /news/article-1081193/Two-years-months-25-days-The-length-time-takes -romance-dead.html?ITO=1490.

4. M. F. Lorber, A. C. Erlanger, R. E. Heyman, and K. D. O'Leary, "The Honeymoon Effect: Does It Exist and Can It Be Predicted?" *The National Center for Biotechnology*, May 2015, https://www.ncbi.nlm.nih.gov/pubmed/24643282?report=abstract.

5. Samantha Joel, "Could You Live Apart, Together?" *Psychology Today*, October 31, 2013, https://www.psychologytoday.com/us/blog/dating-decisions/201310/could -you-live-apart-together

6. Terri Orbuch, "Relationship Rescue: Bringing Back the Passion," *Huffington Post*, July 25, 2012, https://www.huffingtonpost.com/2012/07/25/marriage -counseling-bring-back-passion_n_1695175.html.

7. "Proskollao," Bible Hub, http://biblehub.com/greek/4347.htm.

8. "Dabaq," Bible Hub, http://biblehub.com/hebrew/1692.htm.

9. W. B. Swann, M. J. Gill, "Confidence and Accuracy in Person Perception: Do We Know What We Think We Know about Our Relationship Partners?" *The National Center for Biotechnology*, October 1997, https://www.ncbi.nlm.nih.gov /pubmed/9325592.

10. "Woo," *Wiktionary*, https://en.wiktionary.org/wiki/woo.

11. "Allure," Dictionary.com, http://www.dictionary.com/browse/allured.

12. A. Aron, C. C. Norman, E. N. Aron, C. McKenna, and R. E. Heyman "Couples Shared Participation in Novel and Arousing Activities and Experienced Relationship Quality," *Journal of Personality and Social Psychology*, 78, 2000, 273–284.

13. Vance Fry, "Keep Up the Chase," *Focus on the Family*, December 22, 2016, http://www.focusonthefamily.com/marriage/strengthening-your-marriage/keep -up-the-chase.

CHAPTER 8: SPIRITUAL DISCONNECTION

1. Amanda Green, "10 Monogamous Animals That Just Want to Settle Down," *Mental Floss*, February 4, 2016, http://mentalfloss.com/article/55019 /10-monogamous-animals-just-want-settle-down.

2. Matt Soniak, "The Horrors of Anglerfish Mating," *Mental Floss*, July 22, 2014, http://mentalfloss.com/article/57800/horrors-anglerfish-mating.

3. "Soulmate," *Wikipedia*, https://en.wikipedia.org/wiki/Soulmate.

4. K. G. Kusner, A. Mahoney, K. I. Pargament, and A. DeMaris, "Sanctification of Marriage and Spiritual Intimacy Predicting Observed Marital Interactions across the Transition to Parenthood," *Journal of Family Psychology*, 28 (5), (2014), 604–614.

5. Ibid.

6. Les Parrott and Leslie Parrot, "The Importance of Spiritual Intimacy: Choosing to Believe Together in 2016," *Symbis Assessment*, January 5, 2016, https://www .symbis.com/blog/importance-of-spiritual-intimacy/.

7. Christopher G. Ellison, Amy M. Burdette, W. Bradford Wilcox, "The Couple That Prays Together: Race and Ethnicity, Religion, and Relationship Quality among Working-Age Adults," *Journal of Marriage and Family*, 72 (August 2010): 963-975, http://www.baylorisr.org/wp-content/uploads/wilcox_couplespray.pdf.

8. N. Lambert, F. D. Fincham, N C. DeWall, R. Pond, and S. R. Beach, "Shifting toward Cooperative Tendencies and Forgiveness: How Partner-Focused Prayer Transforms Motivation," *Personal Relationships, 20*(1), (2013),184–197.

9. W. Bradford Wilcox, "Faith and Marriage: Better Together?" *Institute for Family Studies*, July 6, 2017, https://ifstudies.org/blog/faith-and-marriage-better-together.

10. P. R. Amato and S. J. Rogers, "A Longitudinal Study of Marital Problems and Subsequent Divorce," *Journal of Marriage and Family*, 59 (1997): 612–624. See also: W. J. Strawbridge, S. J. Shema, R. D. Cohen, and G. A. Kaplan, "Religious Attendance Increases Survival by Improving and Maintaining Good Health Behaviors, Mental Health, and Social Relationships," *Annals of Behavioral Medicine* 23, no. 1 (2001): 68–74. See also: W. Bradford Wilcox and Nicholas H. Wolfinger, *Soul Mates: Religion, Sex, Love, and Marriage among African Americans and Latinos* (New York: Oxford University Press, 2016).

11. Tyler J. VanderWeele, "Religious Service Attendance, Marriage, and Health," *Institute for Family Studies*, November 29, 2016, https://ifstudies.org/blog /religious-service-attendance-marriage-and-health/.

12. John Skinner, "Marriage and Health Tied to Religious Service Attendance," *Christian Today*, https://christiantoday.com.au/news/marriage-and-health -tied-to-religious-service-attendance.html.

13. "Synergy," *Merriam-Webster*, https://www.merriam-webster.com/dictionary/synergy.

14. Susan Mathis, "Serving Together as a Couple," *Focus on the Family*, January 1, 2011, https://www.focusonthefamily.com/marriage/daily-living/serving-together /serving-together-as-a-couple.

15. Stormie Omartian, *The Power of a Praying Wife* (Harvest House, 2007).

CHAPTER 9: FIGHT FOR US

1. Valerie Peterson, "What You Need to Know about Romance Fiction Genre," *The Balance Careers*, June 25, 2019, https://www.thebalancecareers.com/romance -novels-about-the-romance-fiction-genre-2799896.

2. "Romantic Comedy," *Box Office Mojo*, http://www.boxofficemojo.com/genres/chart /?id=romanticcomedy.htm.

3. Howard J. Markman, Scott M. Stanley, and Susan L. Blumberg, *Fighting for Your Marriage* (Jossey-Bass, 2010), 38.

4. Kyle Benson, "The #1 Thing Couples Fight About," The Gottman Institute, August 5, 2016, https://www.gottman.com/blog/one-thing-couples-fight-about/.

5. "Oppose," *Merriam-Webster,* https://www.merriam-webster.com/dictionary/oppose

6. "Eritheia," Biblehub, http://biblehub.com/greek/2052.htm.

7. "Kenodoxia," Biblehub, http://biblehub.com/greek/2754.htm.

8. "Antidote," *Merriam-Webster*, http://www.merriam-webster.com/dictionary/antidote.

9. "Tapeinoo," Biblehub, http://biblehub.com/greek/5013.htm.

10. "Confirmation bias," *Wikipedia*, https://en.wikipedia.org/wiki/Confirmation_bias.

CHAPTER 10: THE SEXLESS MARRIAGE

1. "The Yada Yada," *Wikipedia*, https://en.wikipedia.org/wiki/The_Yada_Yada.

2. "Yada," Biblehub, http://biblehub.com/hebrew/3045.htm.

3. Diana Appleyard, "How Important Is Sex to a Marriage?" *Daily Mail*, June 23, 2011, http://www.dailymail.co.uk/femail/article-2007065/How-important-sex -marriage-Passion-marriage-wane-So-YOU-making-priority.html.

4. "Clitoris—The Only Organ Designed for Pleasure," *How Stuff Works*, https:// health.howstuffworks.com/sexual-health/female-reproductive-system/clitoris -dictionary1.htm.

5. "Dod," Biblehub, http://biblehub.com/hebrew/1730.htm.

6. "Modern Marriage," Pew Research Center, July 18, 2007, http://www.pewsocialtrends .org/2007/07/18/modern-marriage/.

7. Michele Weiner Davis, *The Sex-Starved Marriage: Boosting Your Marriage Libido*, (Simon & Schuster, 2003), 4.

8. Denise A. Donnelly and Elisabeth O. Burgess, "The Decision to Remain in an Involuntarily Celibate Relationship," *Journal of Marriage and Family*, Vol. 70, No. 2, (May 2008), 519–535.

9. Sharon Jayson, "Sex Survey: What's 'Normal' for Couples?" *USA Today*, January 22, 2013, https://www.usatoday.com/story/news/nation/2013/01/21 /couples-love-sex-relationships/1851965/.

10. Gina Jacobs, "Americans Are Having Sex Less Often, New Study Shows," *Science Daily*, March 7, 2017, https://www.sciencedaily.com/releases/2017 /03/170307112903.htm.

11. Michael Sytsma, "When She Has the Stronger Drive," Building Intimate Marriages, https://intimatemarriage.org/when-she-has-the-stronger-drive/.

12. Sharon Jayson, "Sex Survey: What's 'Normal' for Couples?" *USA Today*, January 22, 2013, https://www.usatoday.com/story/news/nation/2013/01/21/couples-love-sex -relationships/1851965/.

13. Stacey Feintuch and Jacquelyn Cafasso, "Low Sex Drive: Common Causes and Treatment," *Healthline*, https://www.healthline.com/health/low-testosterone /conditions-that-cause-low-libido#sleep.

14. Julie Sprankles, "Are You in a Sexless Marriage? Ways to Tell and How to Fix It, According to an Expert," *ScaryMommy*, http://www.scarymommy.com /sexless-marriage/.

15. Shaunti Feldhahn, *For Women Only: What You Need to Know about the Inner Lives of Men* (Sisters, OR: Multnomah, 2004), 100.

16. Ibid.

17. Seth Stephens-Davidowitz, "Searching for Sex," *New York Times*, January 24, 2015, https://www.nytimes.com/2015/01/25/opinion/sunday/seth-stephens -davidowitz-searching-for-sex.html?_r=0.

18. "How Often Do Americans Have Sex?" *Relationships in America Survey*, The Austin Institute for the Study of Family and Culture, 2014, http://relationships inamerica.com/relationships-and-sex/how-often-do-americans-have-sex.

19. "Couples Who Have Sex Weekly Are Happiest," Society for Personality and Social Psychology, November 17, 2015, http://www.spsp.org/news-center/press -releases/sex-frequency-study.

20. "How Often Do Married Couples Have Sex?" Marriage.com, https://www.marriage .com/advice/physical-intimacy/how-often-do-married-couples-have-sex/.

21. "Low Sex Drive in Women," Mayo Clinic, https://www.mayoclinic.org/diseases -conditions/low-sex-drive-in-women/symptoms-causes/syc-20374554.

22. "Painful Intercourse (Dyspareunia)," Mayo Clinic, https://www.mayoclinic.org /diseases-conditions/painful-intercourse/symptoms-causes/syc-20375967.

23. Cathy Greenblat, "The Salience of Sexuality in the Early Years of Marriage," *Journal of Marriage and the Family*, 45 (1983) 277–288.

24. Joseph Nordqvist, "Erectile Dysfunction Much More Common among Young Men Than Previously Thought," *Medical News Today*, June 9, 2013, https://www .medicalnewstoday.com/articles/261673.php.

25. "More Couples Opting to Sleep in Separate Beds, Study Suggests," CBC, August 6, 2013, http://www.cbc.ca/news/health/more-couples-opting-to-sleep-in-separate -beds-study-suggests-1.1316019.

26. "Restore," *Merriam-Webster*, https://www.merriam-webster.com/dictionary/restore.

27. "Achor," Biblestudytools.com, https://www.biblestudytools.com/dictionary/achor/.

28. "Erect," Dictionary.com, https://www.dictionary.com/browse/erect.

29. Daniel L. Carlson, et al. "The Gendered Division of Housework and Couples' Sexual Relationships: A Reexamination," *Journal of Marriage and Family* (2016), https://onlinelibrary.wiley.com/doi/abs/10.1111/jomf.12313.

30. "Receive," *Merriam-Webster*, https://www.merriam-webster.com/dictionary/receive.

CHAPTER 11: THE CLOSED HEART

1. Archibald D. Hart and Sharon Hart May, *Safe Haven Marriage: Building a Relationship You Want to Come Home To* (Thomas Nelson, 2003) 28.

2. "Hard Hearted," *Thoughts about God*, November 27, 2017, http://thoughts-about -god.com/blog/2011/02/19/ml_hard-hearted/.

3. L. Frank Baum, *The Wonderful Wizard of Oz*, 14.

4. Wayne Blank, "Tearing of Garments," *Daily Bible Study*, http://www.keyway.ca /htm2007/20070313.htm.

5. John Eldredge and Stasi Eldredge, *Love and War: Find Your Way to Something Beautiful in Your Marriage* (Colorado Springs, CO: WaterBrook, 2011), 37.

6. "Patience," *Oxford English Dictionary*, https://en.oxforddictionaries.com/definition /patience.

7. Ashleigh Slater, "4 Proven Ways to Develop Patience with Your Spouse," Crosswalk .com, January 27, 2016, https://www.crosswalk.com/family/marriage/engagement -newlyweds/4-proven-ways-to-develop-patience-with-your-spouse.html.

8. Billy Graham, "The Unmerited Favor of God," Billy Graham Evangelistic Association, https://billygraham.org/devotion/gods-unmerited-favor/.

9. "Grace," *Oxford English Dictionary*, https://en.oxforddictionaries.com/definition /grace.

10. "Gracious," *Merriam-Webster*, https://www.merriam-webster.com/dictionary /gracious.

11. "Compassion," *Wikipedia*, http://en.wikipedia.org/wiki/Compassion.

12. "Decide*," Merriam-Webster*, https://www.merriam-webster.com/dictionary/decide.

13. Angela Duckworth, Christopher Peterson, Michael D. Matthews, and Dennis R. Kelly, "Grit: Perseverance and Passion for Long-Term Goals," *Journal of Personality and Social Psychology*, 92(6):1087-101, July 2007. https://www.researchgate.net /publication/6290064_Grit_Perseverance_and_Passion_for_Long-Term_Goals.

CHAPTER 12: IN OUR WILDEST DREAMS

1. "Synergy," *Oxford English Dictionary*, https://en.oxforddictionaries.com/definition /synergy.

2. "Priscilla and Aquila," *Wikipedia*, https://en.wikipedia.org/wiki/Priscilla_and _Aquila.

CHAPTER 13: THE STORY OF US

1. Kim T. Buehlman, John M. Gottman, and Lynn F. Katz, "How a Couple Views Their Past Predicts Their Future: Predicting Divorce from an Oral History Interview," *Journal of Family Psychology*, Vol. 5(3-4), Mar-Jun 1992, 295-318, https://psycnet.apa.org/doiLanding?doi=10.1037%2F0893-3200.5.3-4.295.

2. Jerry B. Jenkins. *Hedges: Loving Your Marriage Enough to Protect It* (Crossway, 2005), 142.

3. "Get Up on the Wrong Side of the Bed," Idioms Online, https://www.idioms .online/get-up-on-the-wrong-side-of-the-bed/.

4. "Salvage," *Merriam Webster*, https://www.merriam-webster.com/dictionary /salvage.

5. Dave Willis, "The Bigger Story Behind the Story of Your Marriage," *Patheos*. October 30, 2015, http://sixseeds.patheos.com/davewillis/the-bigger-story-behind -the-story-of-your-marriage/.

6. "White Witch," *Wikipedia*, https://en.wikipedia.org/wiki/White_Witch.

7. "After Year of Marriage, Cardi B 'Grew Out of Love,'" *Newser*, December 5, 2018. https://newser.com/s268195.

8. Larry Golkin, "20 Taker Tips," United States Power Squadrons, https://www.usps .org/ventura/art-03-3-tankertips.html.